GRAPHICS CAN BE MANAGED 2

DESIGNERBOOKS

Editor-in-chief: Y&Y (Yang Liu & Jianing Yuan)
Editor: Jingqi Han
Proofreader: Jingqi Han
Art Director: Yannick (Jianing Yuan)
Design Director: Yang Liu
Printing Specialist: Yang Liu
Design and Layout: Jingqi Han, Heng Zhang, Yang Liu

Publisher: DESIGNERBOOKS
Unit D, 16/F, Cheuk Nang 21st Century Plaza, 250 Hennessy Road,
Wanchai, Hong Kong
Tel: +852-2575-5186
Fax: +852-2891-1996
E-mail: edit@designerbooks.com.cn

Distributor: DESIGNERBOOKS
Rm. 504-505, Bld. C, International Negotiate Garden,
NO. 3, Jinguanbei'er Str., Shunyi Dist., Beijing, China
Tel: 0086-10-6400-3080 (Beijing)
　　 0086-21-5596-7639 (Shanghai)
　　 0086-755-8825-0425 (Shenzhen)
　　 0086-20-8756-5010 (Guangzhou)
Fax: 0086-10-64018430-822
E-mail: import01@designerbooks.com.cn
http: //www.designerbooks.com.cn

Printed in China

All rights reserved. No part of this publication may be reproduced in any form or by any means, graphic, electronic or mechanical, including photocopying and recording by an information storage and retrieval system without permission in writing from the publisher.

ISBN: 978-988-77706-3-3
Copyright 2018 © by DESIGNERBOOKS

GRAPHICS CAN BE MANAGED 2

DESIGNERBOOKS

PREFACE

I feel very honor for invited by Designerbooks Publisher, as participant and narrator. In the manuscript offered by the editor, I met a lot of something very familiar, and some of them are my old friends from Behance and Instagram. Compared with "Fantastic Illustration", "Graphic can be Managed" is more like playing, and many artists or designers' works have already been applied into products.

A few years ago, "Transboundary" was a buzzword, while in nowadays, almost everyone is crossing boundary, and a growing number of designers have possessed a series of transformative ability to product innovation, creation, manufacture and display, simultaneously, their expressive form has become diversification and lifestyle. Throughout today, painters in the field of illustration are no longer limited to certain particular style, but often break the single approach that use one kind of material. In short, for the sake of attaining the expectant effect and obtaining wider space and infinite possibility, to widely use all kinds of means is very necessary to the development of illustration.

The development of illustration has a long history, as you and I see, although they seem plain, have profound connotation. On a whole, from the world's oldest cave paintings to Ukiyoe of folk wood block print in Edo age of Japan, every phase demonstrates the progress of illustration. In the early of 1990s, with the coming of illustration art into the era of commercialization as world digital, it plays significant role in promoting economy in market economies, and its concept has gone beyond traditional rules.

I remember that I was invited at last time, I provided as series of works with different styles and more collaborative product (I am "playboy" on art creation), but this time, I make a big subtraction that dig deeper core and greatly strengthen the symbolic expression.

"Flowers" is my (Black Lychee) centerpiece, which started from the first "Maobao" I made it, and I had sent it to my artists' friend as gift. Two years later, I made cooperation on illustration with BVLGARI, Montblanc, Estee

Lauder and Burberry, and after that, I had a strange idea that take only use of 15 flowers to compile a book. For example, I can turn flower into cat, bird, crocodile or else, maybe is a golden star, maybe is the whole universe. Of course, I also try to ask myself, is this a big challenge or a big fun? I think, flower series is the most suitable for the present own after accumulated experience for 20 years. No matter authorized commercial cooperation or exploration of technique, I am the unique one in the world, just be myself.

The book is the crystallization gathering authors' wisdom and creative treasury. Of course, for passers-by out of the field, it is more like a magical world where their souls are led into a broader area.

I will, as always, give my support to the series of book, because in the every book, there have not only a large number of outstanding young writers, but have old drivers waiting for the opportunity.

their own suffering and joy in the nib, and accompanying with pen and paper, to record the most glorious moment and lonely days.

Hei lichee

Website: www.heilichee.com
Weibo: weibo.com/heilichee
WeChat: Heilicheeheilichee

  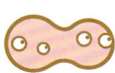  

 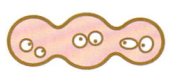   

KIDDD

There is an eidolon with magic strength behind everything in nature. KIDDD advocates the idea of green, natural and healthy teaching. Centered on the core idea of "there is an eidolon behind everything", the brand is designed in shape on the basis of "mountain" that produces everything and refines the cyan from nature symbolizing the flourishing vitality to imply "the pupils surpass the master". In this way, we have formed our exclusive and distinctive vision symbol. The combination of the adorable role design and a rich story-related visual system implies that every ingenious child is an adorable eidolon. They have their own pluses and minuses but with unlimited potential. In addition to the enlightenment in skill, they need to learn how to get along with others and nature in the course of studying and learn to respect and cherish others and nature as a virtue so as to transmit the value of our brand with "love" as the core.

Designer: Susu & Yao
Country: China
Design Agency: 1983ASIA
Creative Director: Susu & Yao
Design Team: SUSU, YAO, XIANG SI

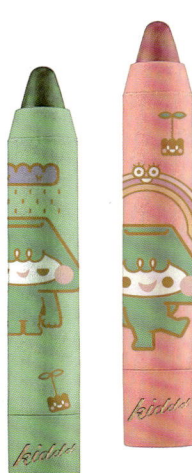

KIDDD

Designer: Susu & Yao
Country: China

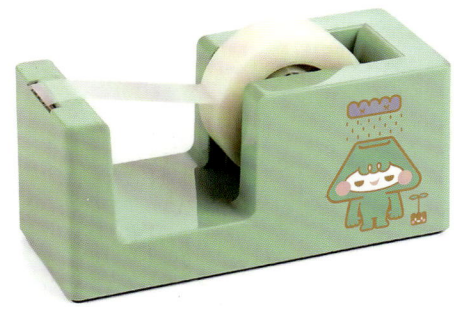

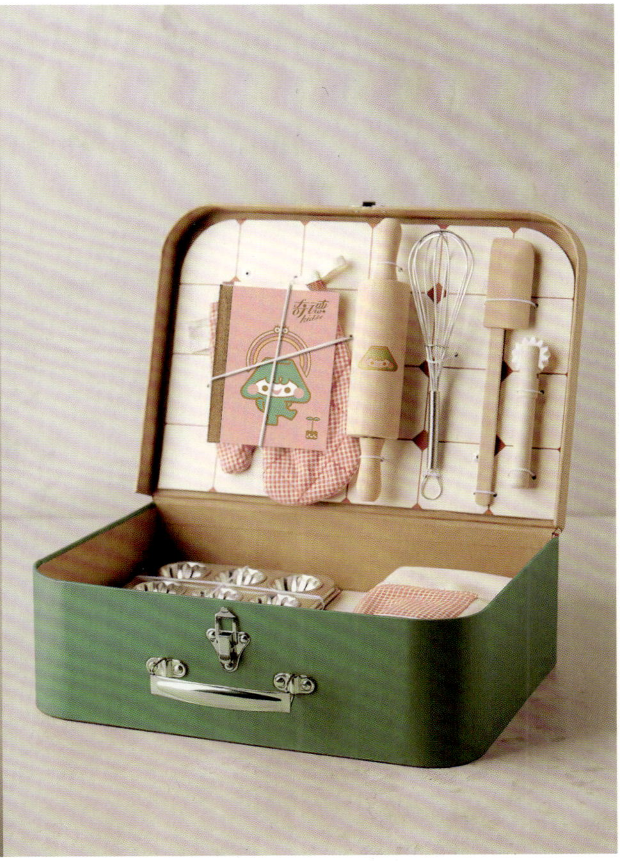

KIDDD

Designer: Susu & Yao
Country: China

kiddd

KIDDD

Designer: Susu & Yao
Country: China

KIDDD

Designer: Susu & Yao
Country: China

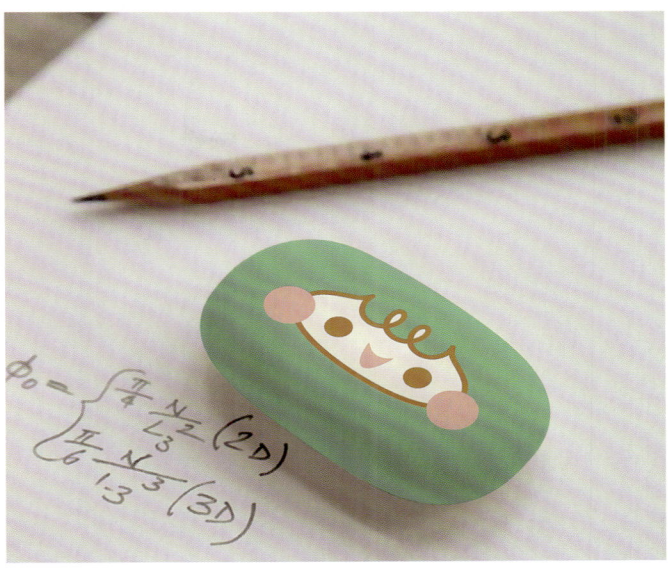

KIDDD

Designer: Susu & Yao
Country: China

CASAHANA

CASAHANA is a food manufacturer of Malaysia specializing in pastries for "festivals and ceremonies". Now it faces the challenge of international brand positioning and younger customer base, and hopes to improve its brand image by branding; therefore, it needs a "universal" story. From its history, we have extracted the concept of "delight & moon". Twelve full moon days not only deliver the brand's original intention of "one ceremony one month" but also serve as the carrier of the brand's diverse development and highlight its unique presence in the marketplace.

Designer: Susu & Yao
Country: China
Design Agency: 1983ASIA
Creative Director: Susu & Yao
Design Team: Susu & Yao

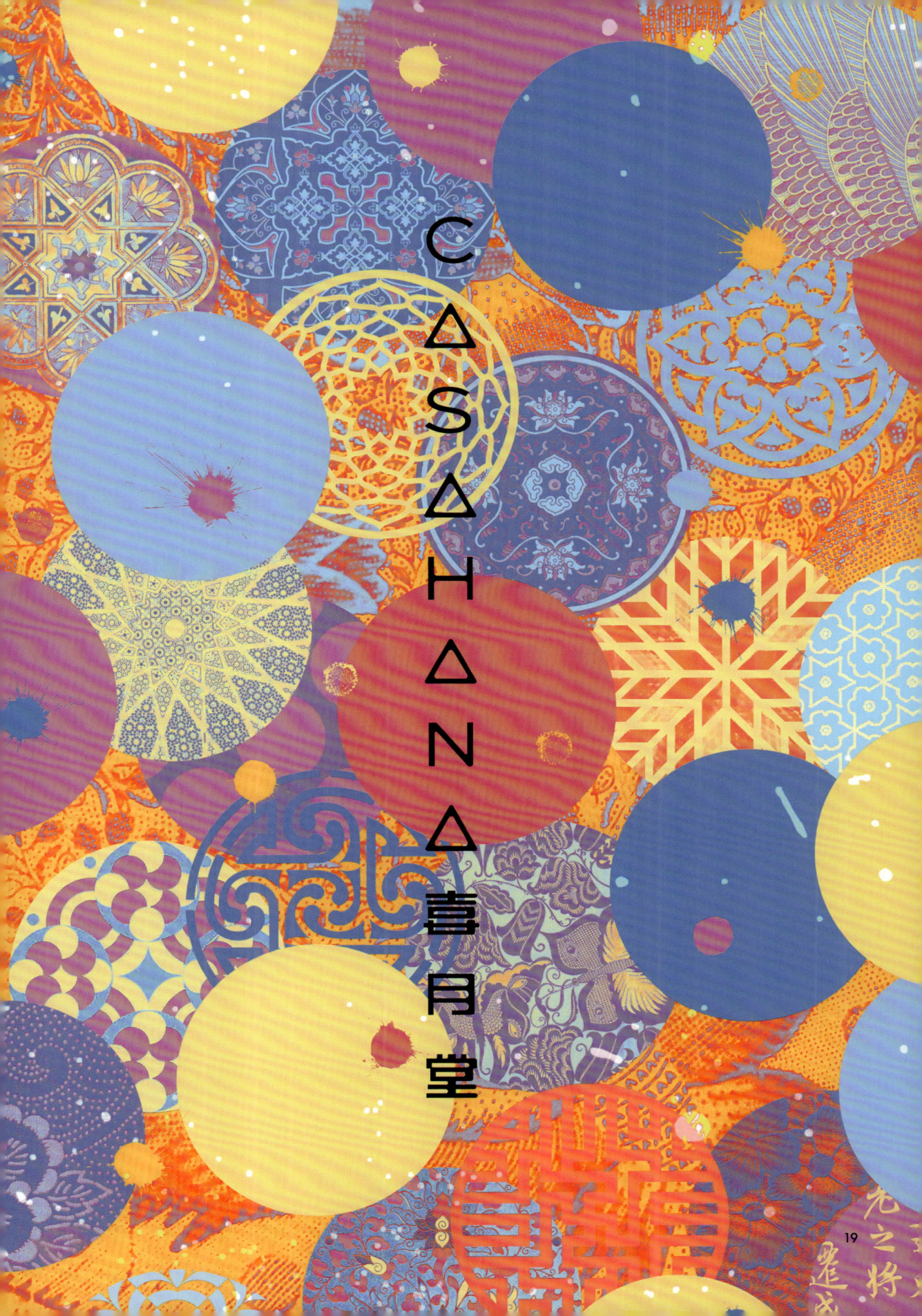

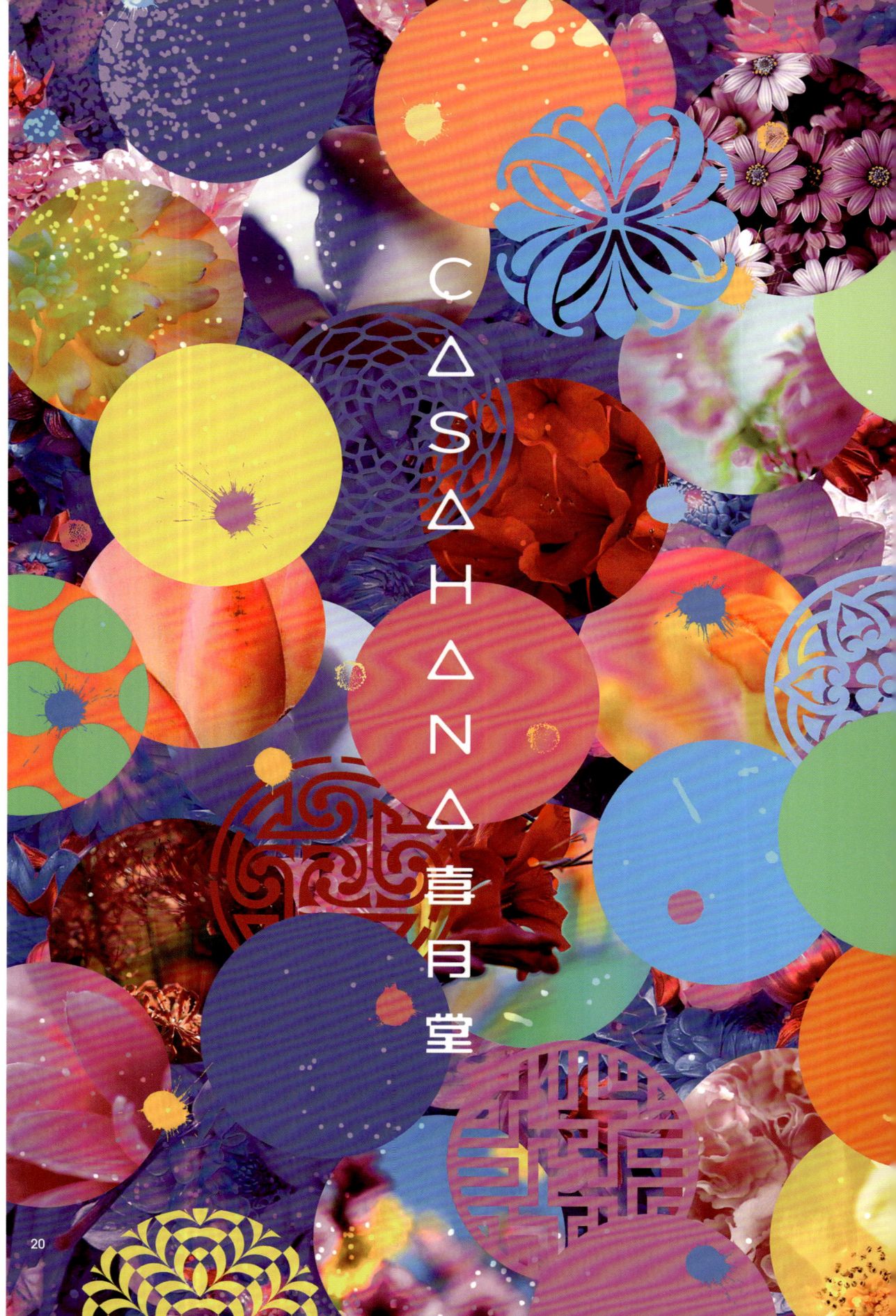

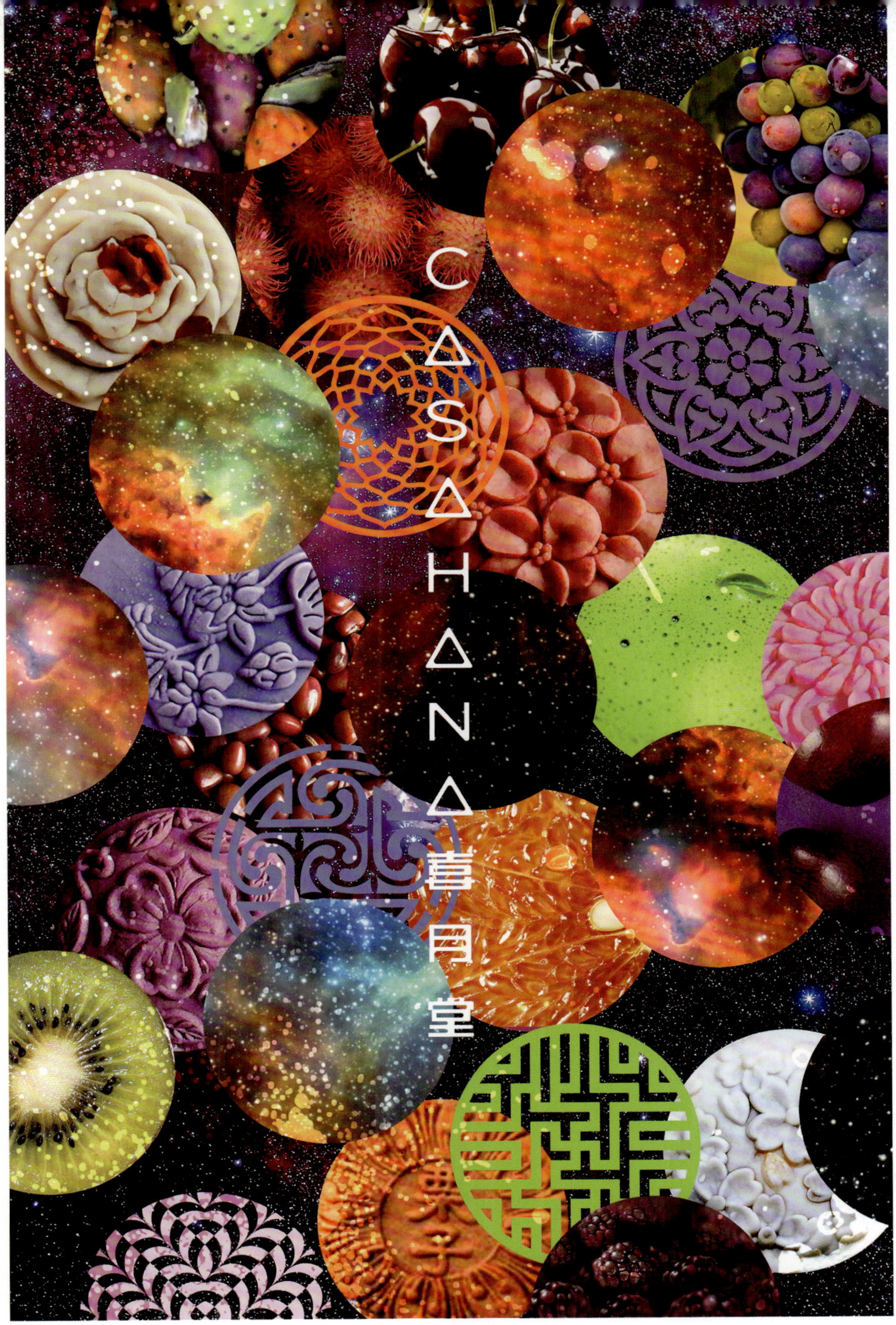

CASAHANA

Designer: Susu & Yao
Country: China

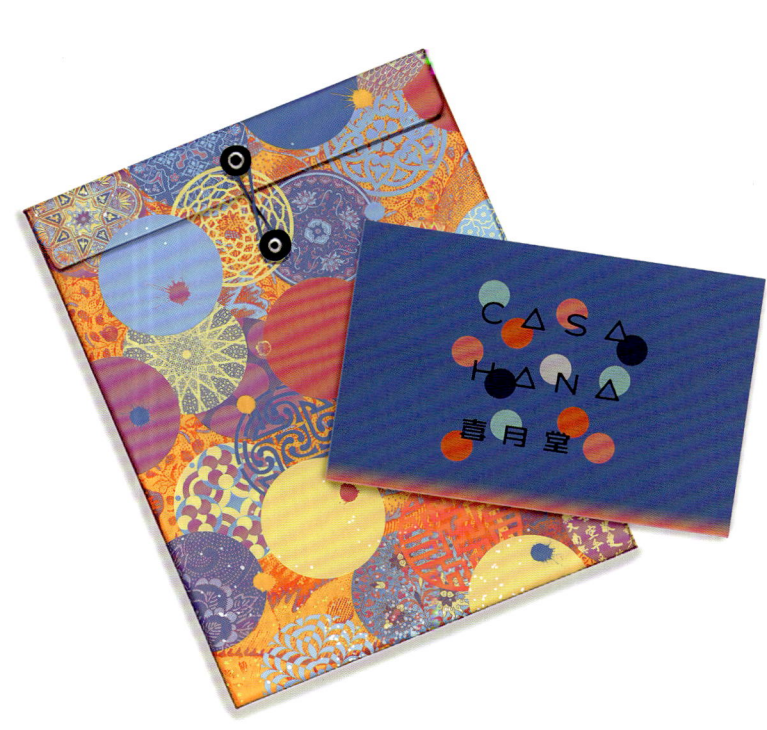

CASAHANA

Designer: Susu & Yao
Country: China

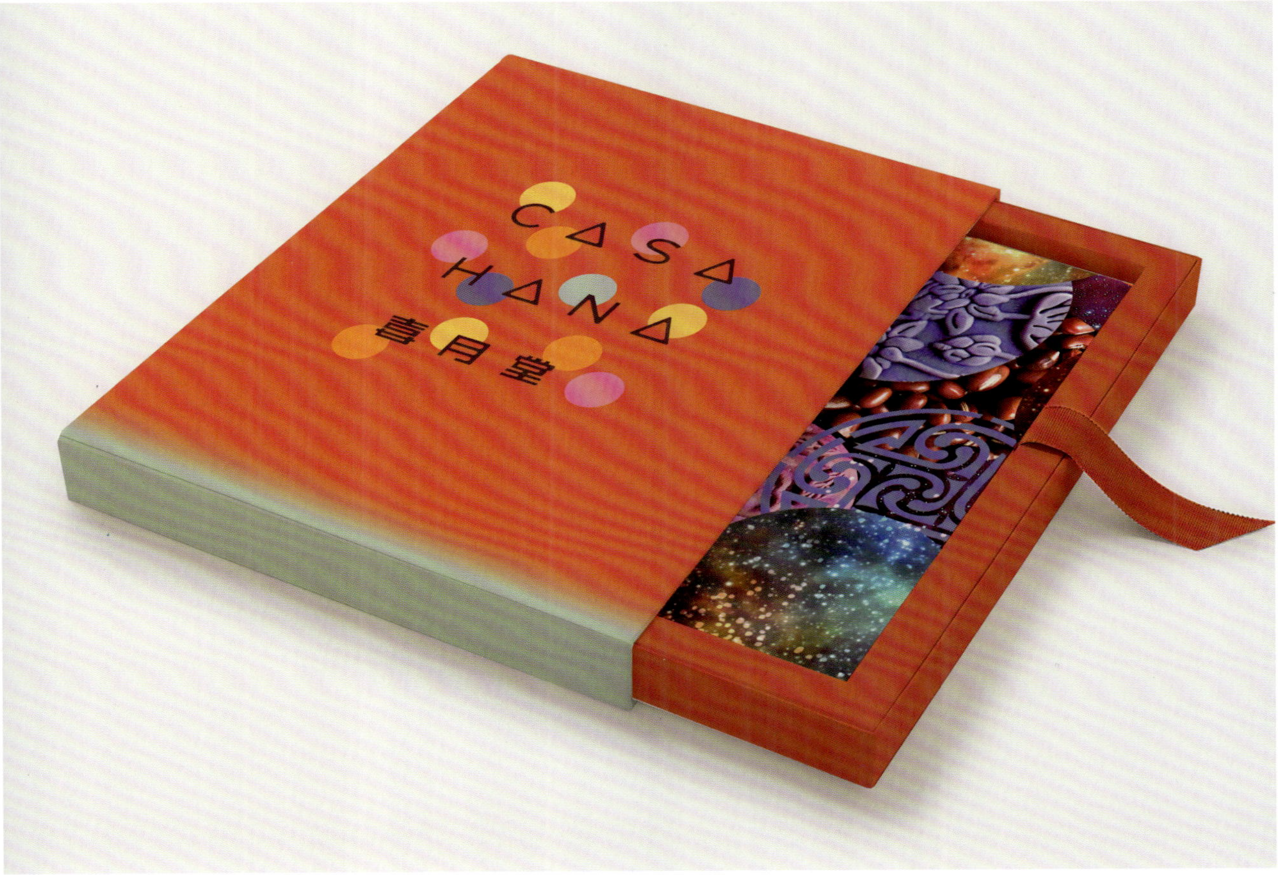

CASAHANA

Designer: Susu & Yao
Country: China

CASAHANA

Designer: Susu & Yao
Country: China

CASAHANA 喜月堂

CASAHANA 喜月堂

CASAHANA

Designer: Susu & Yao
Country: China

CASAHANA

Designer: Susu & Yao
Country: China

CASAHANA

Designer: Susu & Yao
Country: China

CASAHANA

Designer: Susu & Yao
Country: China

KUAS ART CENTER

CULTURE is the memory of life hidden in the blood, the soil nutrient for ART to burgeon. We explore the native cultural icon of Taiwan from an art perspective and extract A (symbol of ART) from ART. By combining the concepts of LIGHT and STAGE, we use the simplified oblique line to manifest the indispensable pureness and spirit of adventure in art creation, and lend more dynamic and active elements to the red color, a color intimately linked to Chinese tradition. For the overall style, the Chinese-English design helps render the complicated yet necessary information in a well-structured manner, and also manages to deliver the dissemination function and aesthetic experience and establish an extendible vision system. In today's globalization, how to maintain territorial distinctiveness and cultural clarity has become a theme requiring our ongoing effort to think over and deal with.

Designer: Susu & Yao
Country: China
Design Agency: 1983ASIA
Creative Director: Susu & Yao
Design Team: Susu, Yao, Fang Yu Qing

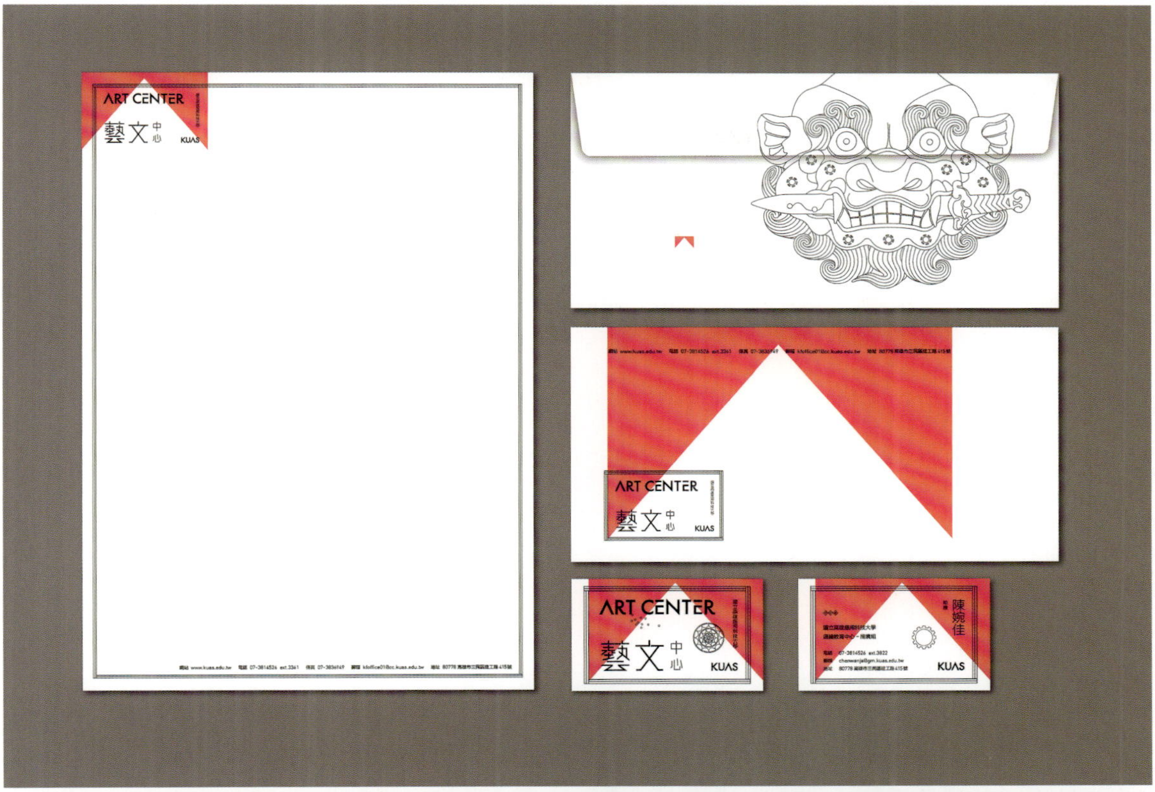

37

KUAS ART CENTER

Designer: Susu & Yao
Country: China

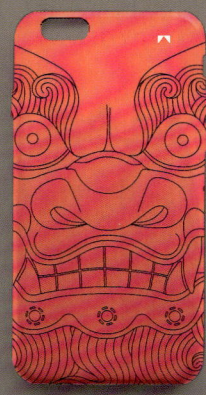

KUAS ART CENTER

Designer: Susu & Yao
Country: China

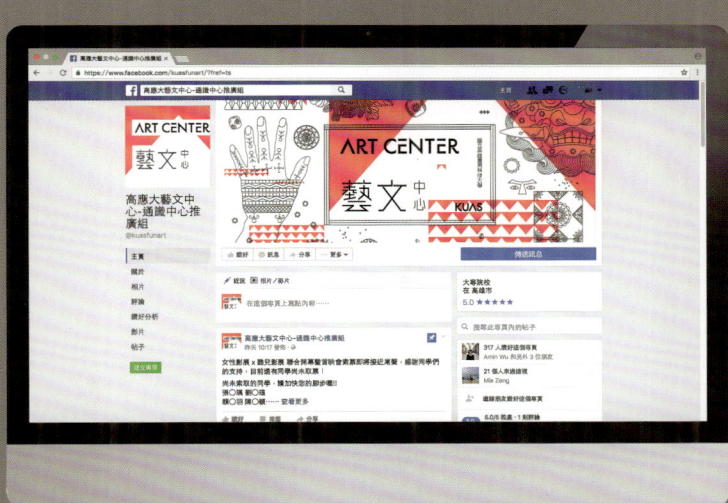

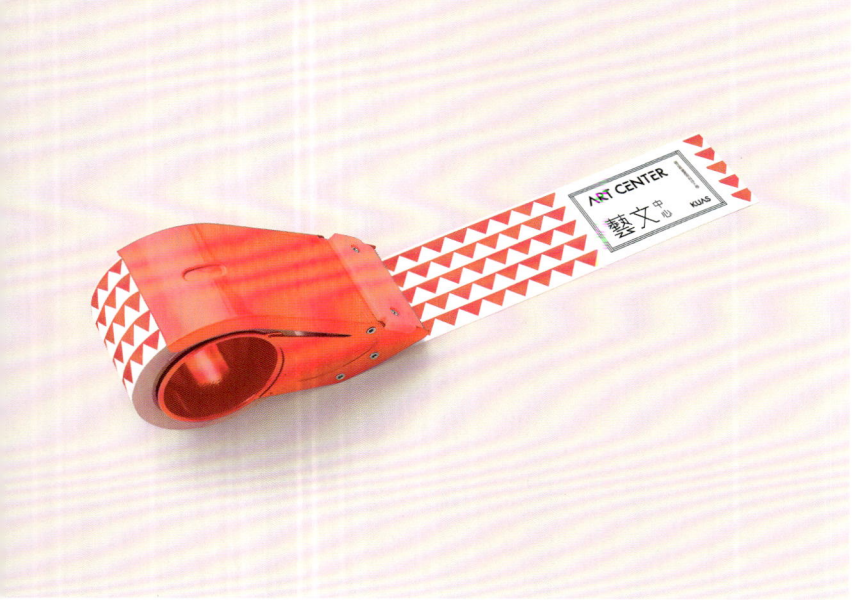

KUAS ART CENTER

Designer: Susu & Yao
Country: China

CENTER OF **GENERAL EDUCATION**

應用科技大學
國立高雄

通識教育中 KUAS

KUAS ART CENTER

Designer: Susu & Yao
Country: China

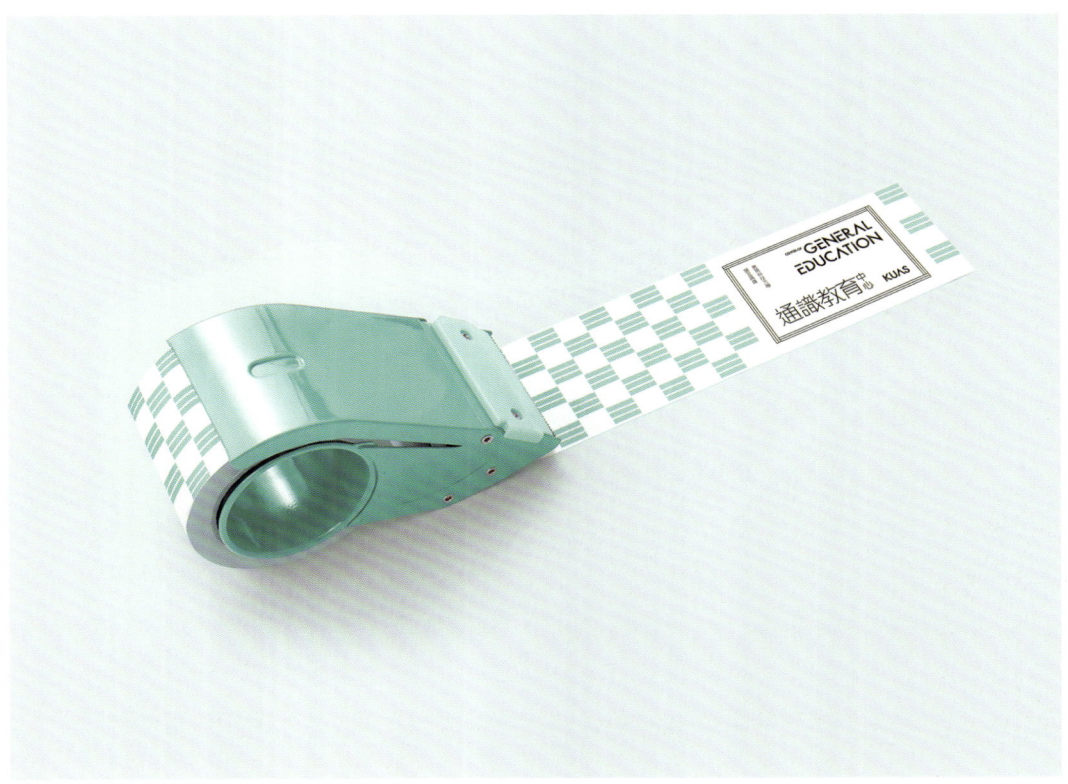

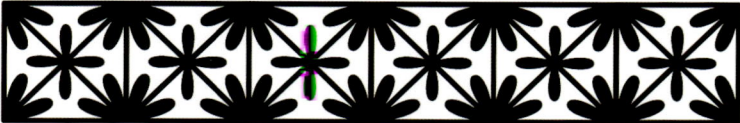

HAAIC

HAAIC is the hotel which integrates the guestroom, catering and business meeting. Explore the local cultural characteristics, and change the hotel into high-star chain hotel as 'cultural hotel' with brand spirit value through our design.1983ASIA examined the local ethnic customs, habits, folk art and daily life architecture of BUYI people with the clients together, in order to find out the totem, valuable color and design system which representative art culture of the BUYI nationality. From these colors and patterns, people may obtain a kind of closely related to the life of pleasure. This is practical emotions.1983ASIA is going to apply this research result to different level of design to the hotel. This will form a strong overall image, which provides various possibilities for the future continuation of the brand. We also hope to take this to bring ancient civilization to the modern life.

Designer: Susu & Yao
Country: China
Design Agency: 1983ASIA
Creative Director: Susu & Yao
Design Team: Susu, Yao, Feng Liang, Chan Hao Mian

HAAIC

Designer: Susu & Yao
Country: China

XINGYI

HAAIC

HOTEL

HAAIC

Designer: Susu & Yao
Country: China

HAAIC

Designer: Susu & Yao
Country: China

HAAIC

Designer: Susu & Yao
Country: China

HAAIC

Designer: Susu & Yao
Country: China

HAAIC

Designer: Susu & Yao
Country: China

61

HAAIC

Designer: Susu & Yao
Country: China

HAAIC

Designer: Susu & Yao
Country: China

HAAIC

Designer: Susu & Yao
Country: China

HAAIC

Designer: Susu & Yao
Country: China

HAAIC

Designer: Susu & Yao
Country: China

HAAIC

Designer: Susu & Yao
Country: China

HAAIC

Designer: Susu & Yao
Country: China

P

Gmund Urban

Equipped with state-of-the-art materiality, we were allowed to create our idea of urbanity in the form of a work tool. The basic concept of the design is the element of the line, which links all design disciplines in the modern living space – regardless of whether we speak of architecture, interior design or product design. The line connects things or excludes them, the spaces in between are filled with building materials. The elected typography establishes the second level for us and the line is only then able to display its true character in the presence of the information level. We opted for a Neuzeit Grotesk font for titles, headlines and notes. The lower case "r" was modified for titles and headlines. The colour scheme is monochrome and is accented with hot foil in copper. A slipcase, which also serves as the cover of a drawer, holds a sample book and image brochure. The folding boxes that reside in the drawer are filled with the original material inspirations, wood and cement. Samples from the entire paper collection can be found in a Hakoya Box, produced for GMUND in Japan. All elements of the set feature a variety of printing and finishing processes. We transferred the design system back to the cityscape. Two trade fair stands were constructed for Packaging Innovations London and for Luxe Pack in Monaco. We consider this work tool an invitation to the recipient to design his own personal urbanity; to continue the line, pursue perspectives and connections – or choose to have it end abruptly.

Designer Max Kuehne
Country: Germany
Design Agency: Paperlux GmbH
Creative Director: Max Kuehne
Art Director: Daniela Gilsdorf
Client: Büttenpapierfabrik Gmund
Photographer: Michael Pfeiffer

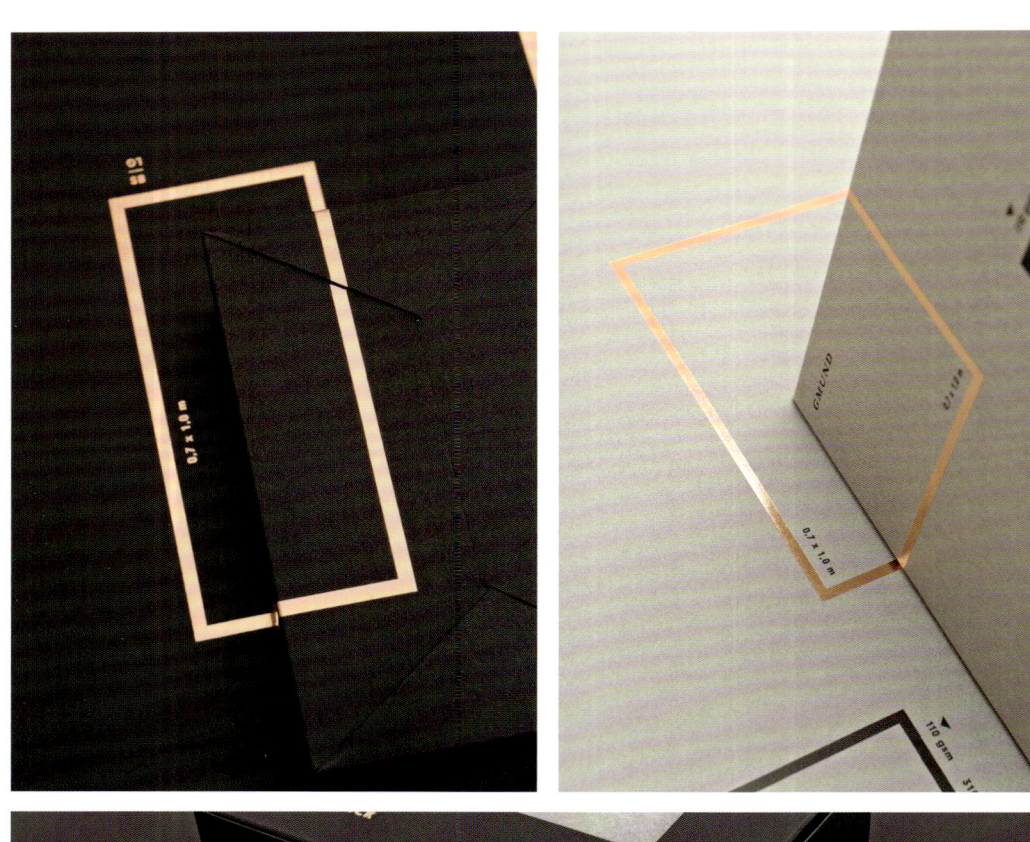

Gmund Urban

Designer Max Kuehne
Country: Germany

les contrebandiers

Inspired by the period of the prohibition, Quebec's Contrebandiers whiskey is proposed hidden inside a solid block of wood from which we can extract the bottle with a thinny red thread. The bottle is wrapped in a map to follow the path of the Montreal smugglers to the United States. The brand using the raccoon with his masked bandit air evokes this very common rodent that is about everywhere in Quebec, even in cities.

Designer: Maxime Archambault
Country: Canada
Photographer: Jana Taillade

THE THING t-shirt — 4 DIMENTION

t-shirt illustration around the theme off the 4 dimensional.

Designer: Maxime Archambault
Country: Canada
Photographer: Bruno Berthelet
Client: THE THING

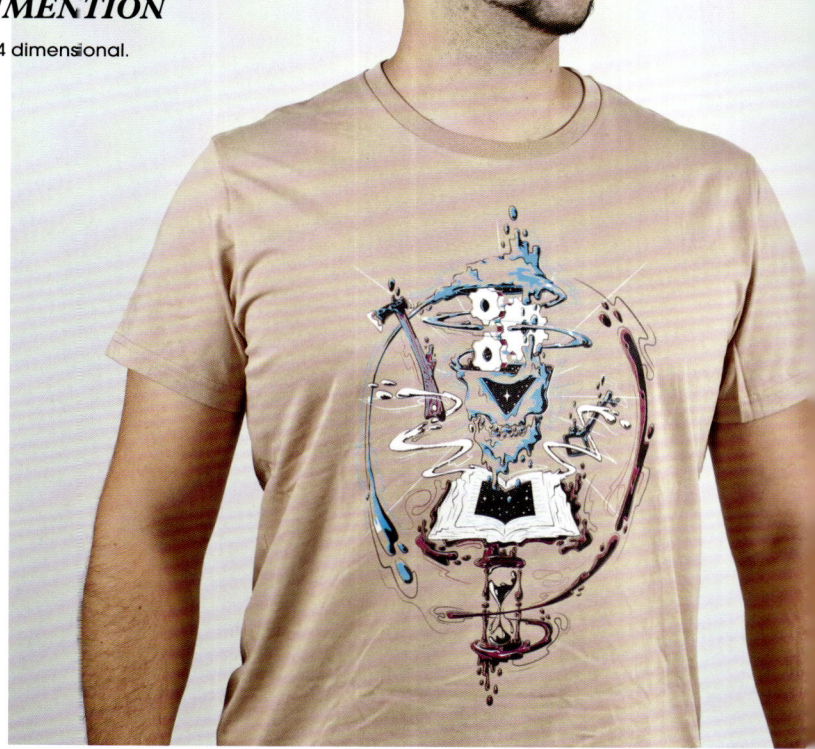

83

THE THING t-shirt — 4 DIMENTION

Designer: Maxime Archambault
Country: Canada

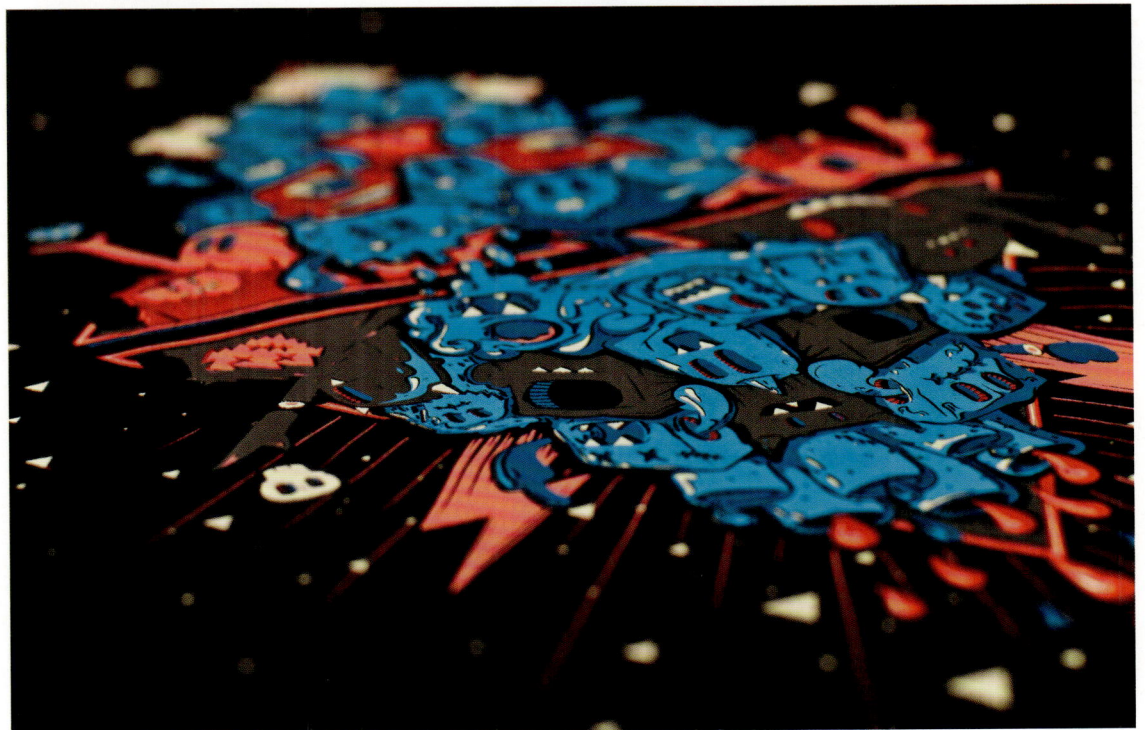

THE THING t-shirt — 4 DIMENTION
Designer: Maxime Archambault
Country: Canada

THE THING t-shirt

Designer: Maxime Archambault
Country: Canada
Photographer: Bruno Berthelet
Client: THE THING

Animals tangled lines

Designer: Anna Kozlenko
Country: Ukraine

Asia set

Designer: Anna Kozlenko
Country: Ukraine

Christmas collection

Designer: Anna Kozlenko
Country: Ukraine

MERRY CHRISTMAS
— FLAT ICONS —

Christmas flat symbols

Christmas silhouettes

Designer: Anna Kozlenko
Country: Ukraine

Coffee animals stains

Designer: Anna Kozlenko
Country: Ukraine

Silhouette city

Watercolor food logos

Designer: Anna Kozlenko
Country: Ukraine

Running food & drink

~ Orange TEA ~

~ Vanilla TEA ~

~ Orange TEA ~

~ Green TEA ~

~ White TEA ~

~ Mint TEA ~

~ Hibiscus TEA ~

° Lemon TEA °

Watercolor Tea Menu

Designer: Anna Kozlenko
Country: Ukraine

Miss Mushy

Miss Mushy, a group of ladies, lives in an unnoticeable and subtle corner. They speak the same language; they hold the same beliefs. Although they are a unique species, divergence manifest among individuals including personalities, interests, fashions and thoughts. Ceci wishes people believe that there are different flocks of creatures, which are invisible in human life. We live in the same world; they, unfortunately, are out of sight, out of mind.

Designer: Ceci Lam
Country: Hong Kong, China

Miss Mushy

Designer: Ceci Lam
Country: Hong Kong, China

Crystal World

Designer: Ceci Lam
Country: Hong Kong, China

Crystal World

Designer: Ceci Lam
Country: Hong Kong, China

Serendipity Travel

Designer: Ceci Lam
Country: Hong Kong, China

114

The Original design Calendar of Guoguan

Chinese traditional culture about the wisdom of throttle custom and living custom, we have inherited and presented them in the works, 12 months-12 illustrations, nearly a thousand of cultural elements into the works, which can be graffiti color, postcard to share your blessing, or mount into the picture to collect the time. A warm cultural calendar, to describe every day with you in 2017.

Design Agency: Guangzhou Guoguan Culture Communication Co., Ltd.
Country: China
Creative Director: Penny Peng
Art Director: TT Wong
Photographer: Louis Leo
Designer: Darren Yiu
Client: Guoguan
Photographer: Louis Leo

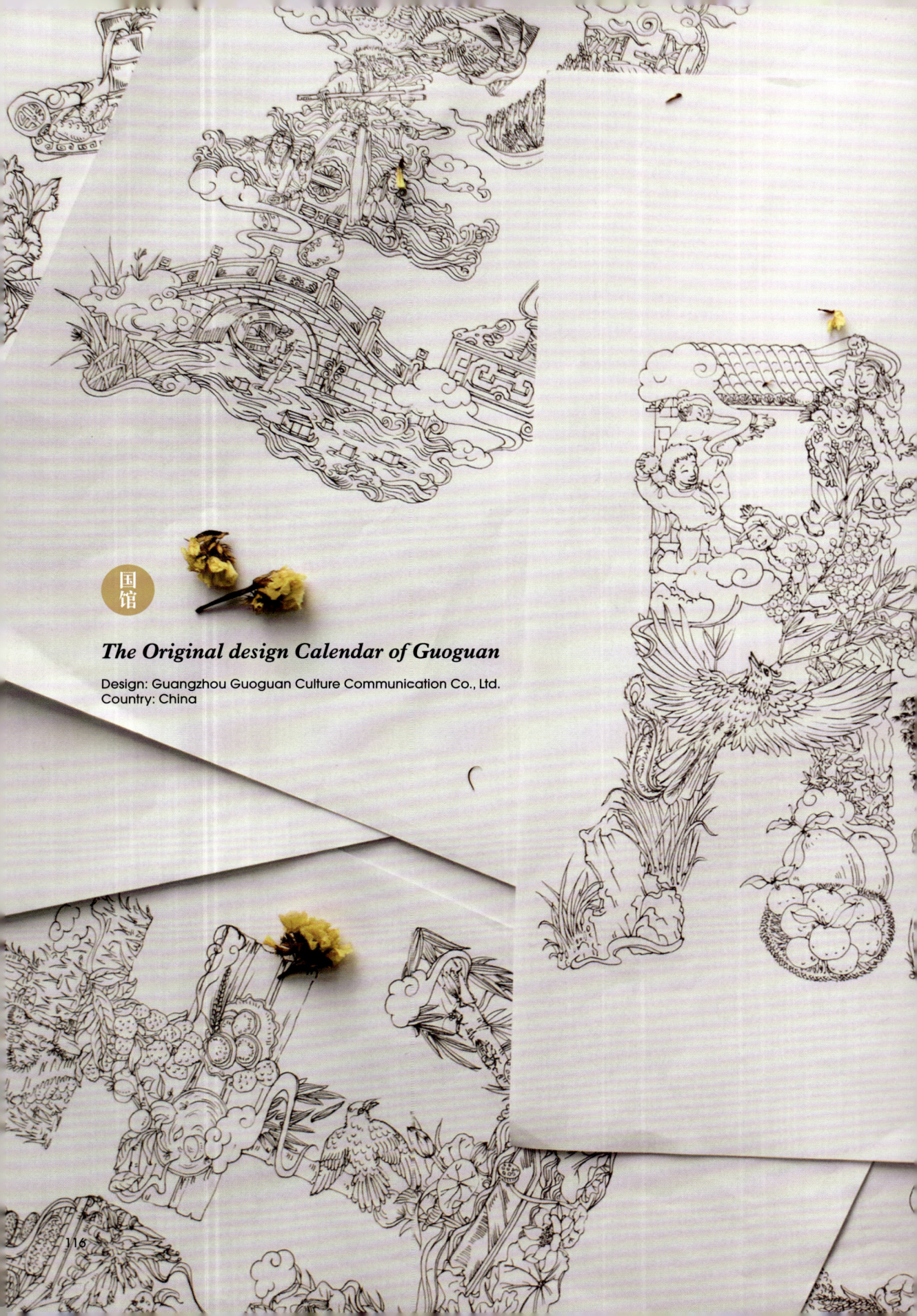

国馆

The Original design Calendar of Guoguan

Design: Guangzhou Guoguan Culture Communication Co., Ltd.
Country: China

118

国馆

The Original design Calendar of Guoguan

Design: Guangzhou Guoguan Culture Communication Co., Ltd.
Country: China

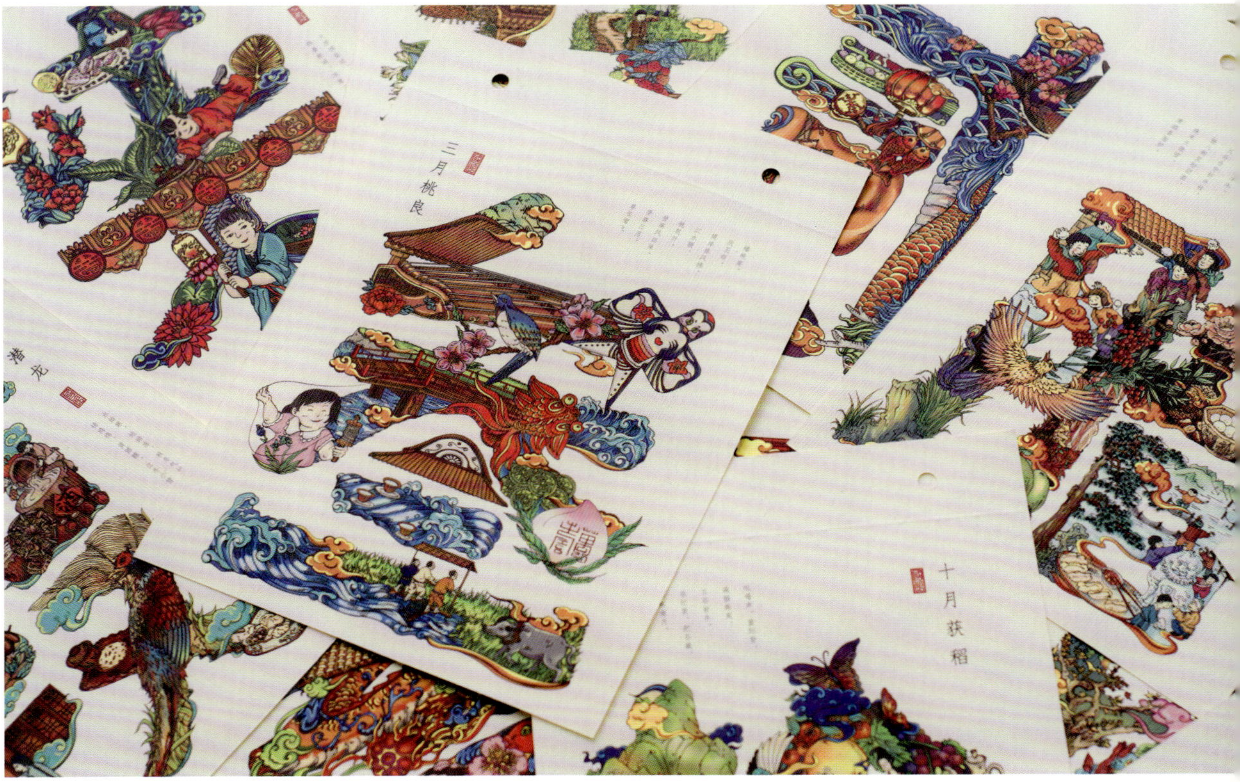

The Original design Calendar of Guoguan

Design: Guangzhou Guoguan Culture Communication Co., Ltd.
Country: China

122

国馆

The Original design Calendar of Guoguan

Design: Guangzhou Guoguan Culture Communication Co., Ltd.
Country: China

CATSTRONAUT

The Freaky Bus

Fancy a Creep-pa?

Designer: Beatrice Tinarelli
Country: Italy

SCHOOL TIME

PARTY QUOTES

Designer: Beatrice Tinarelli
Country: Italy

che fretta c'era
Maledetta Primavera

HELLO MARINE!

Designer: Beatrice Tinarelli
Country: Italy

MONSTERS

the Old Woman who lived in a Shoe

Designer: Beatrice Tinarelli
Country: Italy

HELLO FOOD!

PATTERNS

Designer: Beatrice Tinarelli
Country: Italy

Aloha Lolligag

Lolligag is a character designed by Fantastic Bombastic Inc. Every year this brand designs a new Lolligag binyl toy model, to invite fomus artisrs around the world to make some cool art and to create a new version of the doll.

Designer: Jhonny Núñez
Country: Colombia
Design Agency: Jhonny Núñez - Studio
Creative Director: Charles O'connor
Art Director: Jhonny Núñez
Client: Bombastic FantasticInc.

Códice Azteca

Chcuerías de Arte is a publishing house from Sapin, they are constanlty interested on found new amzing illustrator and artisits to createbooks, this one is Códice Azteca, a book that featured the many kinds of demigods from the Aztec culture.

Designer: Jhonny Núñez
Country: Colombia
Design Agency: Chucherías de Arte Pulishing
Creative Director: Seferino López
Art Director: Jhonny Núñez
Client: Cucherías de Arte
Video: Seferino López

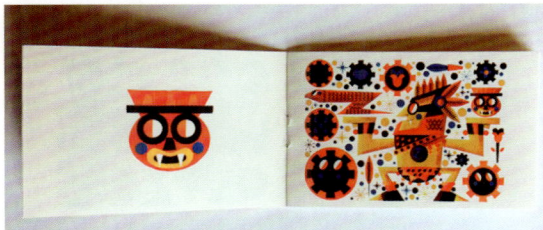
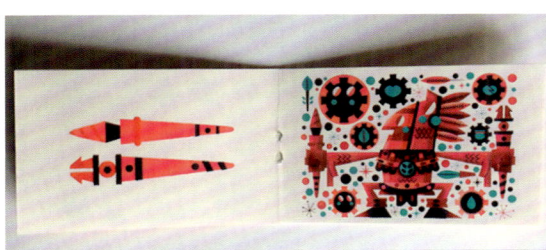

Códice Azteca

Designer: Jhonny Núñez
Country: Colombia

Light and Darkness

Lolligag is a character designed by Fantastic Bombastic Inc. Every year this brand designs a new Lolligag binyl toy model, to invite fomus artisits around the world to make some cool art and to create a new version of the doll.

Designer: Jhonny Núñez
Country: Colombia
Design Agency: Jhonny Núñez - Studio
Creative Director: Charles O'connor
Art Director: Jhonny Núñez
Client: Bombastic FantasticInc.

Los Hombres Sin Alma

Cover illustration for the book "Los Hombres sin alam" (The Men Without Soul).

Designer: Jhonny Núñez
Country: Colombia

Selk'nam

Cover illustration for New Poetry Magazin.

Rolltop Nº 90

Manufraktura is an independet bran from Slovenia, focus on create new models of accesories and backpacks, they hired me to create an amazing new style of backpack decorate with my illustrations on it, the topic is the fairy tales.

Designer: Jhonny Núñez
Country: Colombia
Design Agency: Jhonny Núñez - Studio
Creative Director: Katerina Marai
Art Director: Jhonny Núñez
Client: Manufraktura

Pool 2016 calendar

a personal project calendar Aditya Pratama created about swiming pool.

Designer: Aditya Pratama (sarkodit)
Country: Indonesia

Berrybenka collector`s edition box

Berrybenka is an online fashion store that offers clothing, foot wear and accessories for men and women, and Aditya Pratama (sarkodit) made the illustration for Berrybenka collector`s edition box 4th year anniversary

Designer: Aditya Pratama (sarkodit)
Country: Indonesia
Client: Berrybenka

Berrybenka collector`s edition box

Designer: Aditya Pratama (sarkodit)
Country: Indonesia

"Stay" wall art

The wall art Aditya Pratama created for Yats Colony hotel. YATS Colony is a multiple and inclusive collection of memories. It is a home for a hotel, a bistro, a boutique and a collaborative working space, built from the compassion of the founding family. Location : Jl. Patangpuluhan No.23, Patangpuluhan, Wirobrajan, Yogyakarta, Indonesia.

85 cm

69 cm

1

66 cm

54 cm

3

47 cm

66 cm

2

43 cm

43 cm

4

Designer: Aditya Pratama (sarkodit)
Country: Indonesia
Client: Yats Colony Hotel

"Stay" wall art

TDesigner: Aditya Pratama (sarkodit)
Country: Indonesia

12 Masters

I was selected as one of illustrators for Star Wars Weekend Art Project, an tribute exhibition for Star Wars, supported by Disney Indonesia. I illustrated 12 Jedi masters with my own style.

Designer: Tommy Chandra
Country: Indonesia

Astronaut/Cosmonaut

Submission for Poolga in 2013, site that provides art for iphone, ipad and ipod. I picked the space theme. Inspired by David Bowie's Space Oddity, i made 2 illustrations – Astronaut for girl and Cosmonaut for boy. In 2016, i recolored the illustrations with the pantone vibrant colors.

Designer: Tommy Chandra
Country: Indonesia
Client: poolga

Crossing Boundaries: New Voices from Indonesia

1 main illustrations, 9 editorial illustrations. ABC RN, in partnership with Arts Centre Melbourne, presents Crossing Boundaries: New Voices from Indonesia, an anthology of new Indonesian writing from across the archipelago – Bali, Java, Sumatra and Sulawesi. The project involves the publication of nine Indonesian short stories, translated from various Indonesian languages into English, presented in both written and audio format.

Designer: Tommy Chandra
Country: Indonesia
Client: ABC RN

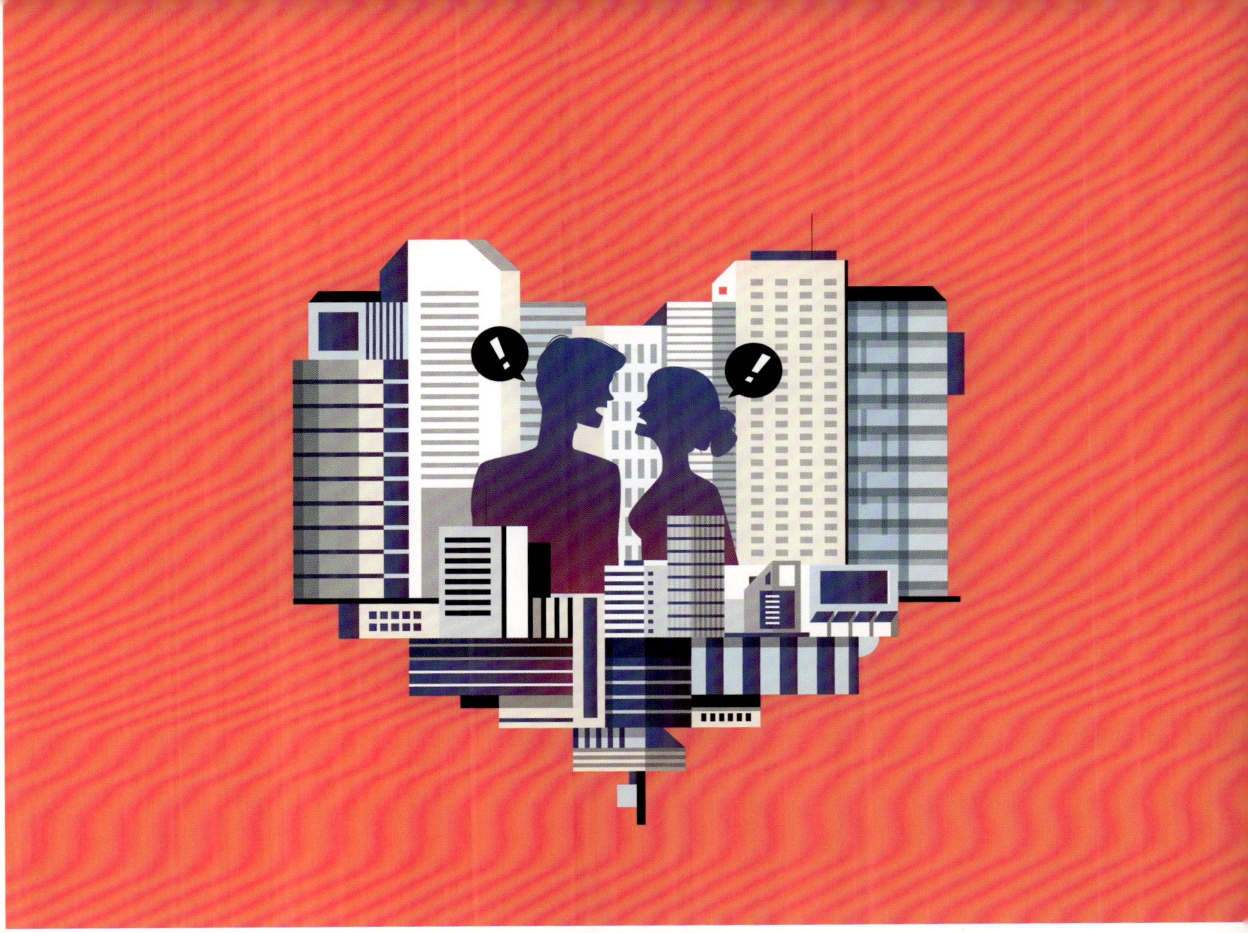

157

Crossing Boundaries: New Voices from Indonesia

Designer: Tommy Chandra
Country: Indonesia

ELLE Shopping

A series of editorial illustrations for ELLE Shopping magazine . I illustrated some fashion items, furnitures, cosmetics and other woman stuffs for this magazine. I also did the cover, a collage of other stuffs that formed an illustration of a bag.

Designer: Tommy Chandra
Country: Indonesia
Client: ELLE Indonesia

ELLE Shopping

Designer: Tommy Chandra
Country: Indonesia

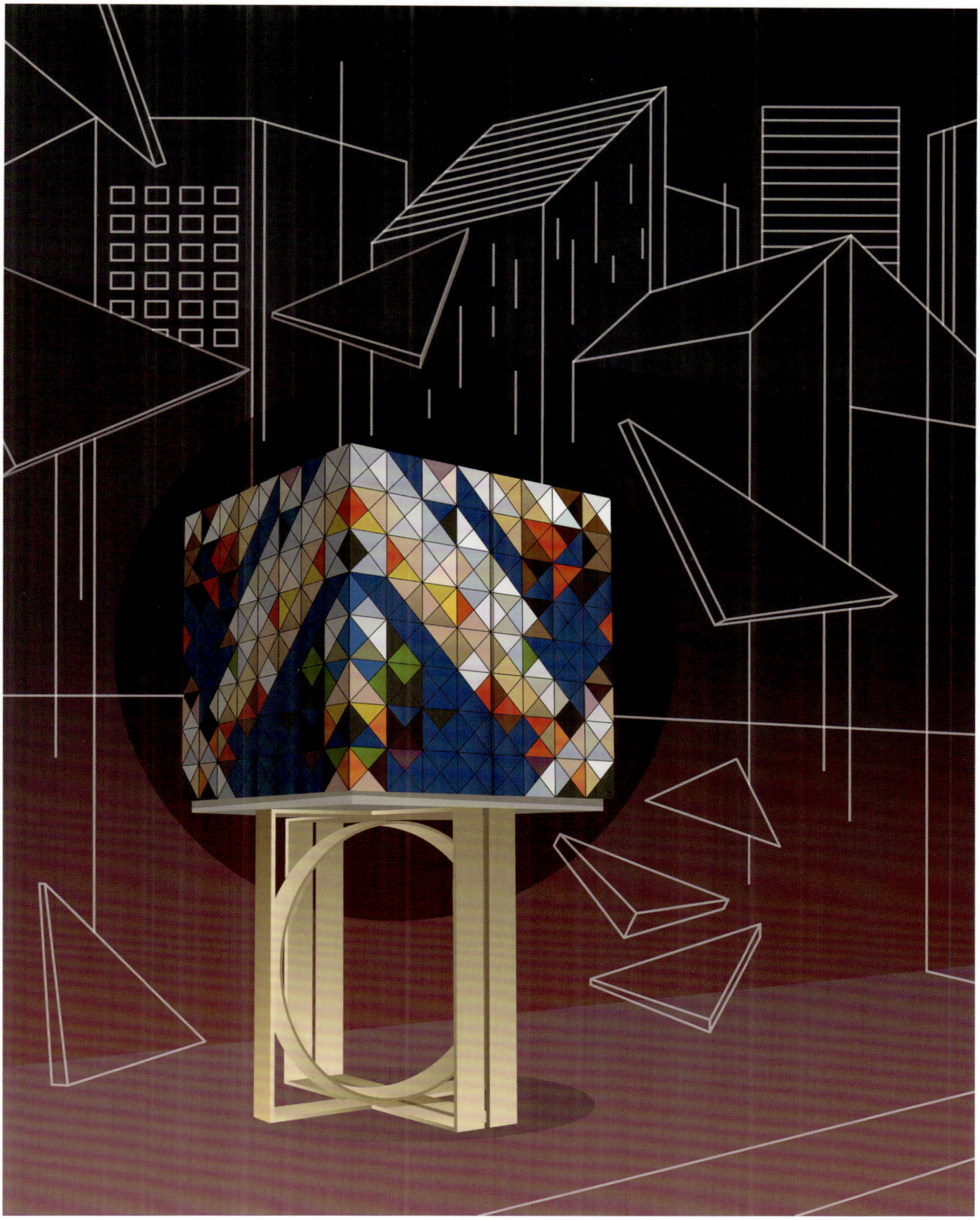

A Love Letter for Jakarta

Commission posters for An anthology movie – A Love Letter for Jakarta (Surat Cinta untuk Jakarta), supported by Governor of Jakarta and Jakarta Art Council. The movie consisted of 3 short movies about Jakarta from different perspectives. I made 2 alternative posters for the movie.

SURAT CINTA UNTUK JAKARTA

Designer: Tommy Chandra
Country: Indonesia
Client: Jakarta Art Council

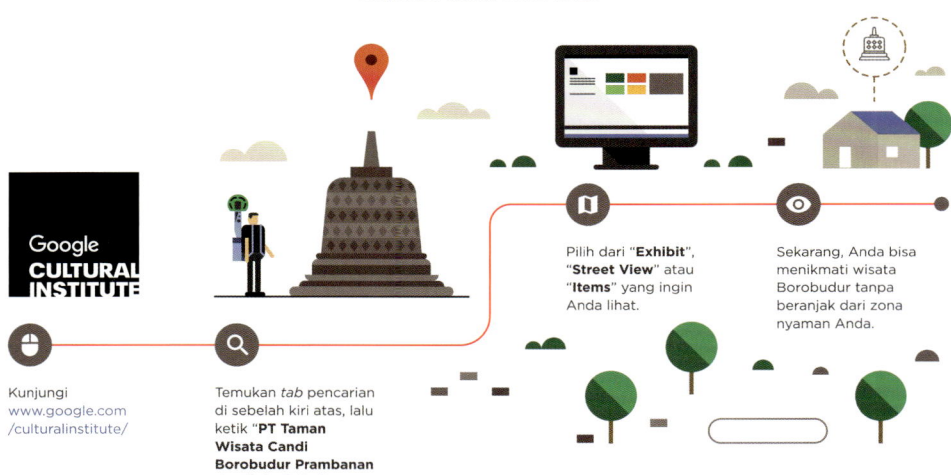

Google Indonesia calendar 2016

Design and illustration for Google Indonesia calendar 2016 (printed version). Google Indonesia wanted their products showed in the calendar each month. The products were illustrated as infographics, so the calendar receivers (client/partners/others) could understand and had the basic informations about the products. Each illustration used simple form and colors.

Voice Search

Mengizinkan pengguna untuk menggunakan Google Search dengan berbicara di ponsel pintar atau komputer

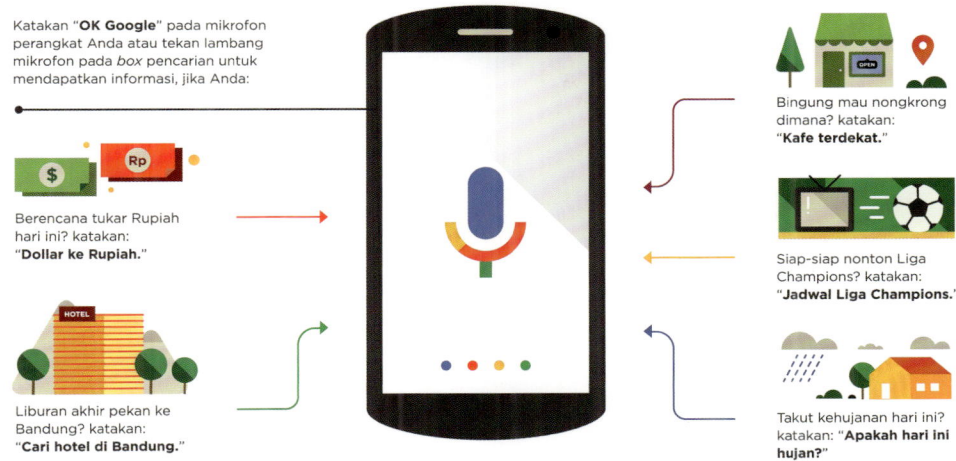

Katakan "**OK Google**" pada mikrofon perangkat Anda atau tekan lambang mikrofon pada *box* pencarian untuk mendapatkan informasi, jika Anda:

Berencana tukar Rupiah hari ini? katakan: "**Dollar ke Rupiah.**"

Liburan akhir pekan ke Bandung? katakan: "**Cari hotel di Bandung.**"

Bingung mau nongkrong dimana? katakan: "**Kafe terdekat.**"

Siap-siap nonton Liga Champions? katakan: "**Jadwal Liga Champions.**"

Takut kehujanan hari ini? katakan: "**Apakah hari ini hujan?**"

Google Maps Offline

Mencari dan navigasi arah di Google Maps tanpa koneksi Internet

Buka aplikasi **Google Maps** di ponsel Anda, ketik nama wilayah yang Anda tuju.

Ketik nama wilayah di kotak putih paling bawah, kemudian pilih "**Download**".

Setelah mengunduh peta yang Anda pilih, **Google Maps** akan tetap bekerja tanpa koneksi Internet.

Designer: Tommy Chandra
Country: Indonesia
Client: GOOGLE Indonesia

Monster buddies

This art is known as "Doodle Art" wich is a mix of furny colorful cartoon characters and shapes.

Designer: Reda El Mraki
Country: UK

Monster buddies

Designer: Reda El Mraki
Country: UK

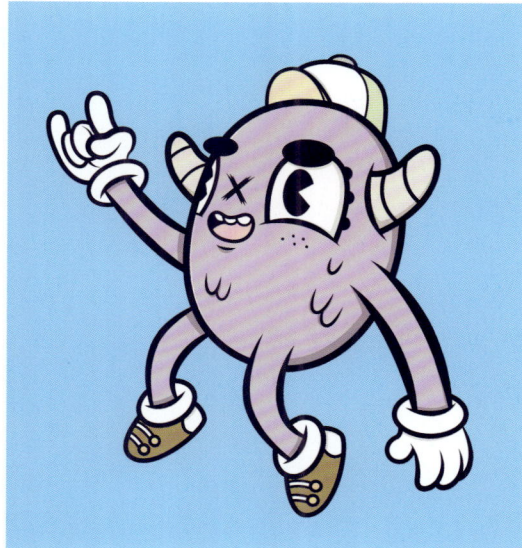

Monster buddies

Designer: Reda El Mraki
Country: UK

Boathouses

This is a self-initiated series of boathouses which is inspired by the cozy floating houses in the canals of Amsterdam.

Designer: Rutger Paulusse
Country: Netherlands

Boathouses

Designer: Rutger Paulusse
Country: Netherlands

Cabinet

This is a self-initiated illustration, based around the theme 'seeing'. The idea of this piece was inspired by 'cabinets of curiosity'.

Designer: Rutger Paulusse
Country: Netherlands

Monstera

This illustration is a tribute to one of the hippest plants of the moment, combined with the most famous Dutch flower; the tulip.

GS1

Rutger was approached by creative agency Leftloft to create illustrations for the annual report of GS1. The idea was to visualize logistics, based around the theme of an abstract factory.

Designer: Rutger Paulusse
Country: Netherlands
Client: GS1

Camper

When Rutger went on an epic road trip with his lovely girlfriend, he was inspired to make this illustration. On their trip they were traveling around Europe in a campervan. Fully equipped, so they could keep freelancing and enjoying the good life from their mobile home.

Designer: Rutger Paulusse
Country: Netherlands

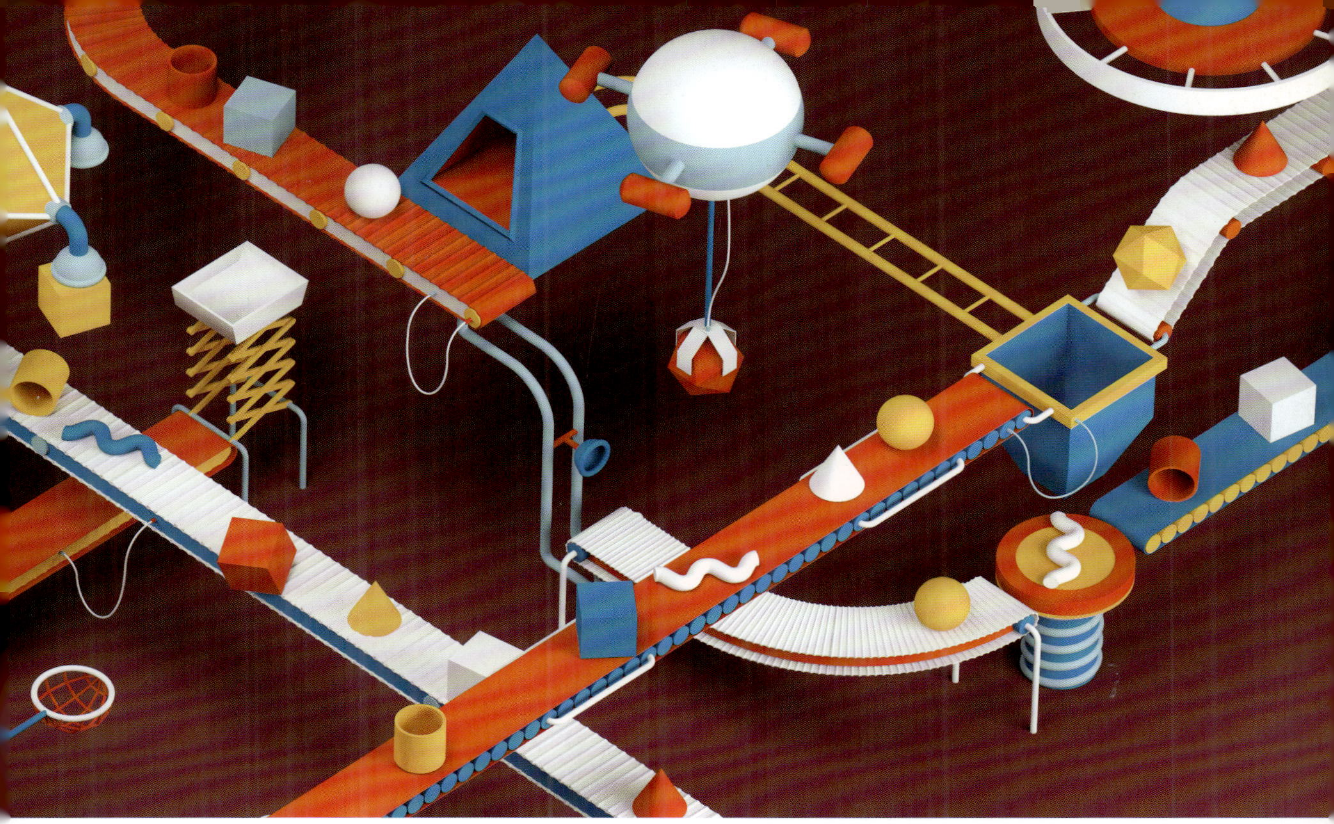

Hero

Rutger was approached to illustrate how Hero makes their jam in this fun infographic.
The illustration is going to be used internal for educational purposes.

Designer: Rutger Paulusse
Country: Netherlands
Design Agency: Vormers'vuur
Client: Hero

Join Up

This typographic illustration was made for a collaboration with Room CR6 from London, they animated this piece about meeting new people and create stuff together even if you have never met in real life.

Designer: Rutger Paulusse
Country: Netherlands
Creative Director: Rutger Paulusse & Room CR6
Client: Hero

Layover With A Local

Rutger teamed up with Achtung! to create the key visual and some city maps for a new campaign for KLM; Layover With A Local. People travelling to Amsterdam can meet-up with a local to change the usually boring layover time to a moment to experience this amazing city. Achtung! created an app to make this awesome idea come to life.

Designer: Rutger Paulusse
Country: Netherlands
Design Agency: Achtung!
Creative Director: Daniel Sytsma
Client: KLM
Characters: Scott Mcpherson

Van Gansewinkel

Rutger was asked to create two infographics for Van Gansewinkel's new website
One is about how waste doesn't really exist, which takes you through all the steps of recycling waste and Van Gansewinkel's workflow. The second one is about the production of a self developed product which makes products such as tiles for pavement out of waste.

Designer: Rutger Paulusse
Country: Netherlands
Client: Van Gansewinkel

Van Gansewinkel

Designer: Rutger Paulusse
Country: Netherlands

CITIx60 City

Whether it's a one-day stopover or a longer trip, CITIx60 is your inspirational guide. Initiated and edited by viction:ary, the pocket-sized collection sports an artistic edge with a handpicked list of hotspots loved by 60 stars of the cities' creative scene.

Illustrator: Guillaume Kashima
Country: France
Client: viction:ary, Hong Kong.

CITIx60 City

Illustrator: Guillaume Kashima
Country: France

Gourmie's Japanese Classics vol.3

Culinary fanzine by japanese chef Fumiko Suzuki (Gourmie) and Guillaume kashima. Riso printed in Flat Gold and Teal. Cover with Metallic Gold. 20 pages, A5, fotokarton black + munken print papers.

Illustrator: Guillaume Kashima
Country: France

DIE BESTEN KARTEN FÜR DEN ECHO 2013

Wir gratulieren unseren ECHO Nominierten und ECHO Gewinnern:

ASAF AVIDAN & THE MOJOS • BRUCE SPRINGSTEEN • BUSHIDO • FANTASY
GOSSIP • GREGORIAN • HEINO • JOE COCKER • MICHAEL HIRTE • MICHAEL WENDLER
MRS. GREENBIRD • OLAF • PETER MAFFAY • P!NK • SILBERMOND

www.sonymusic.de

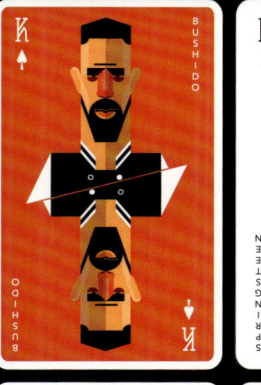
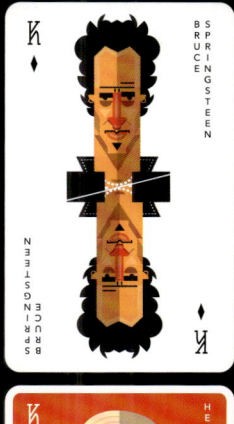
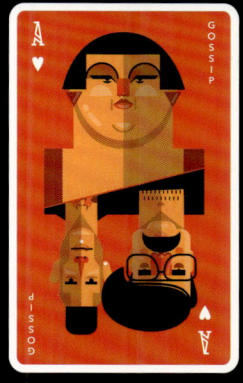
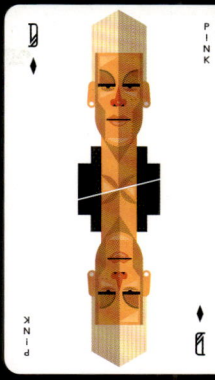
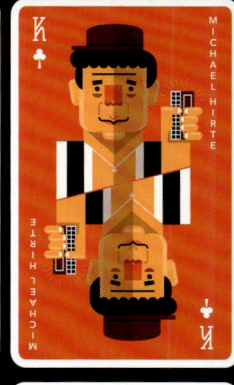

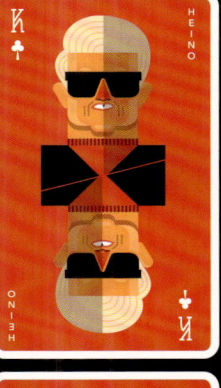
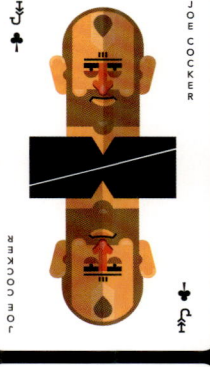
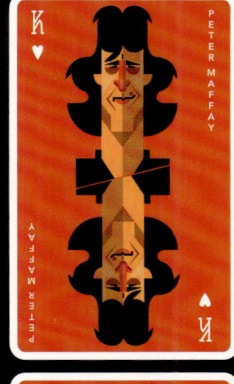
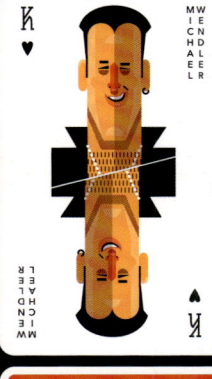
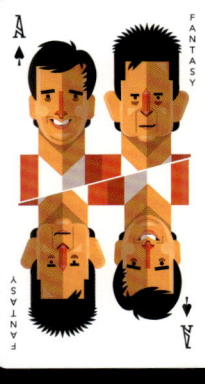
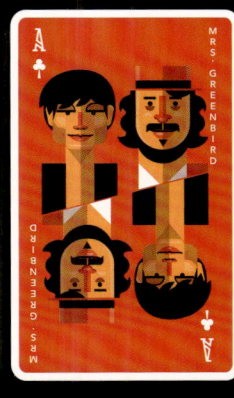
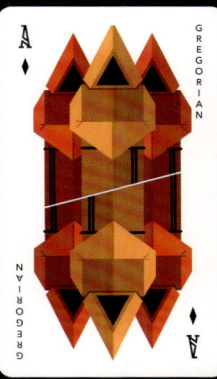
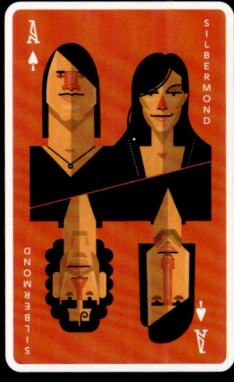
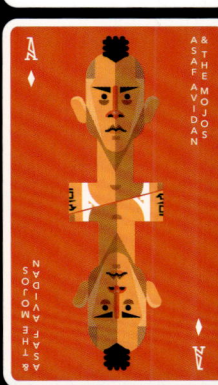

Sony Music - Echo

Sony Music asked Musclebeaver to design an advertisement to thank their Echo Award nominated artists.
The caricatured international stars were put into a set of poker cards.
The advertisement title says: "The best cards for the Echo 2013".

Designer: Musclebeaver
Country: Germany
Design Agency: Musclebeaver
Client: Sony Music Germany

KUONI elsewhere

Illustrated fun facts about different international countries and travel destinations for the travel agency Kuoni Switzerland.

Designer: Musclebeaver - Andreas Kronbeck
Country: Germany
Design Agency: Büroecco Kommunikationsdesign GmbH
Client: KUONI

KUONI *elsewhere*

Designer: Musclebeaver - Andreas Kronbeck
Country: Germany

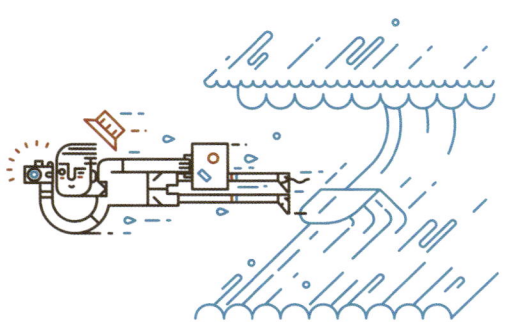

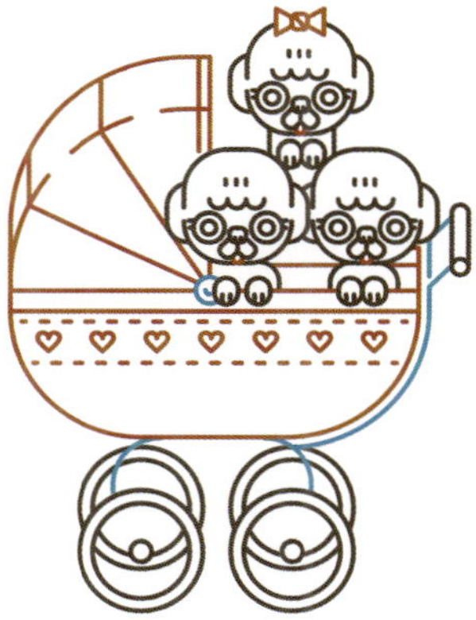

KUONI elsewhere

Designer: Musclebeaver - Andreas Kronbeck
Country: Germany

KUONI elsewhere

Designer: Musclebeaver - Andreas Kronbeck
Country: Germany

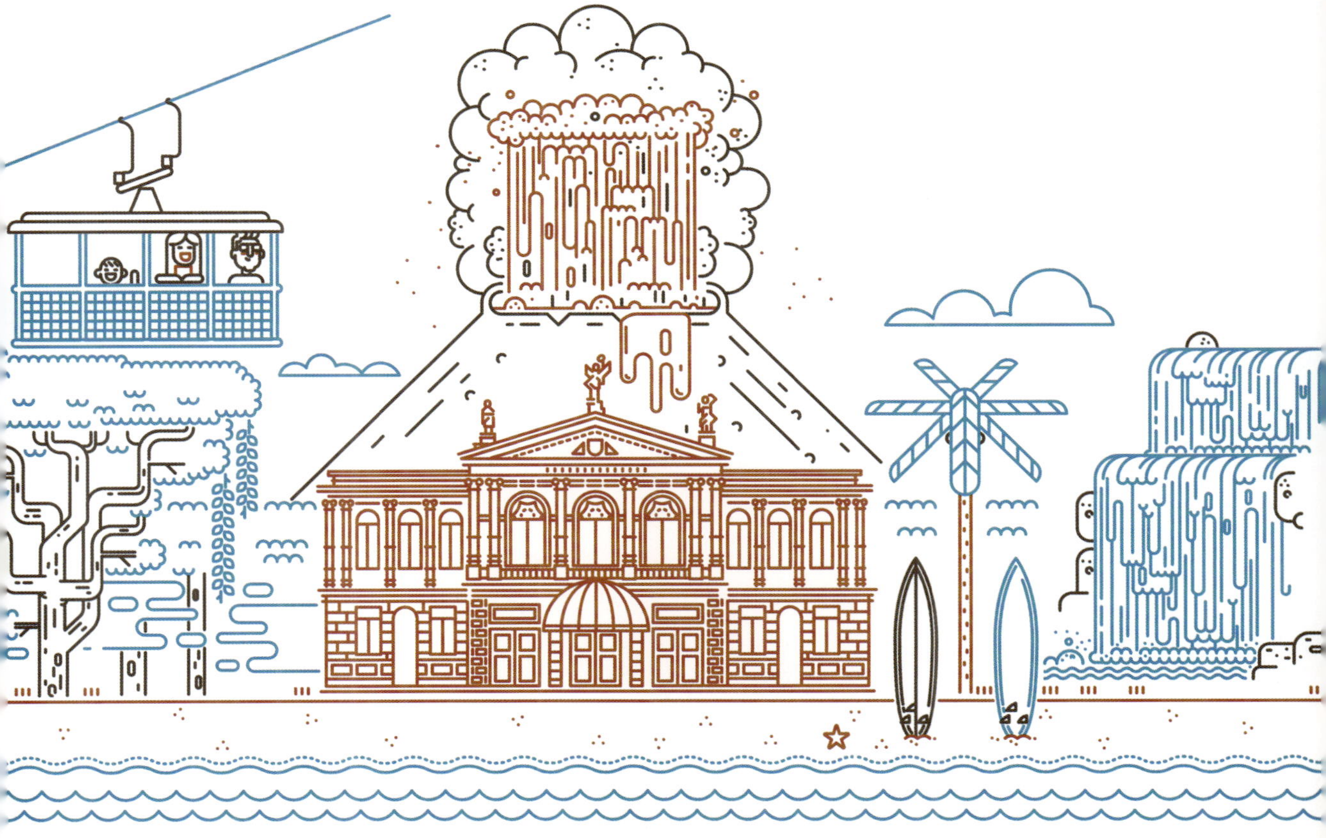

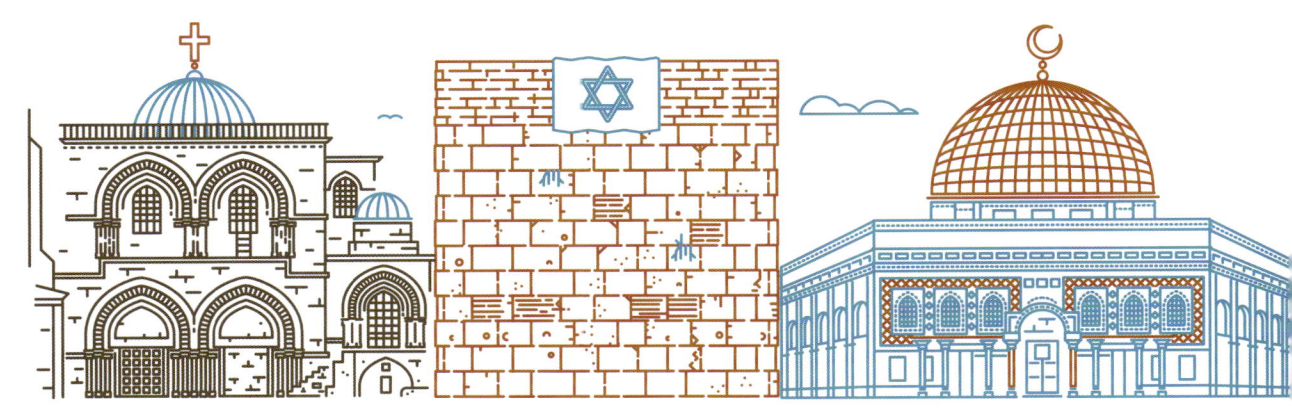

KUONI *elsewhere*

Designer: Musclebeaver - Andreas Kronbeck
Country: Germany

KUONI *elsewhere*

Designer: Musclebeaver - Andreas Kronbeck
Country: Germany

KUONI *elsewhere*

Designer: Musclebeaver - Andreas Kronbeck
Country: Germany

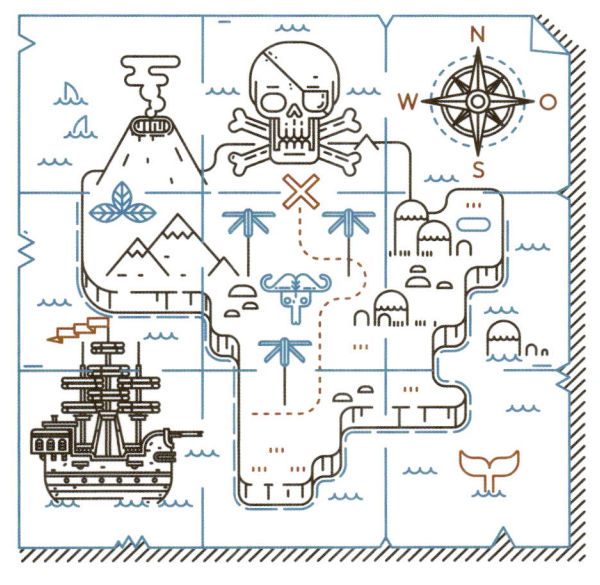

214

KUONI *elsewhere*

Designer: Musclebeaver - Andreas Kronbeck
Country: Germany

KUONI elsewhere

Designer: Musclebeaver - Andreas Kronbeck
Country: Germany

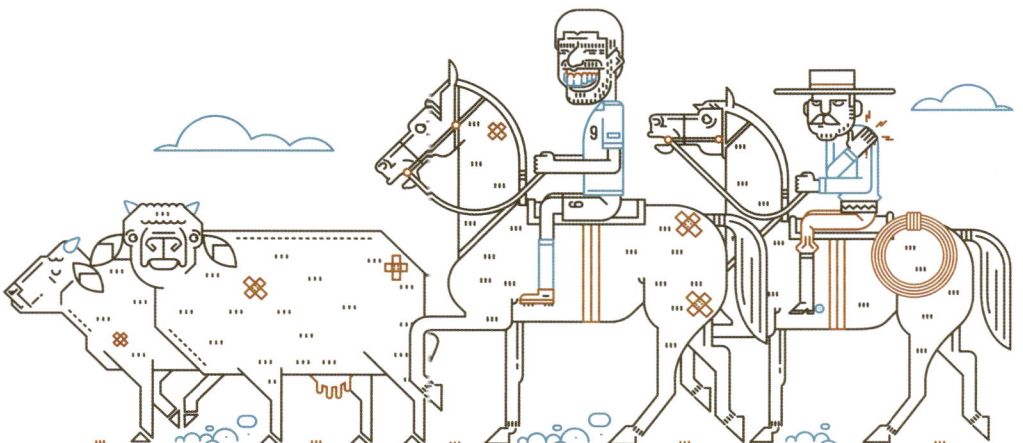

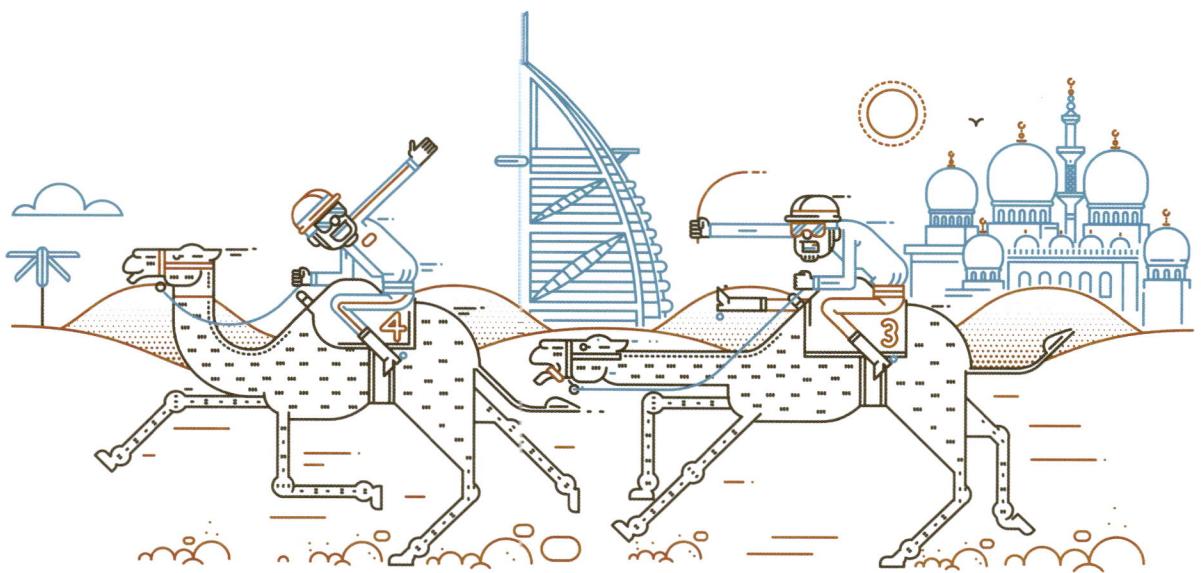

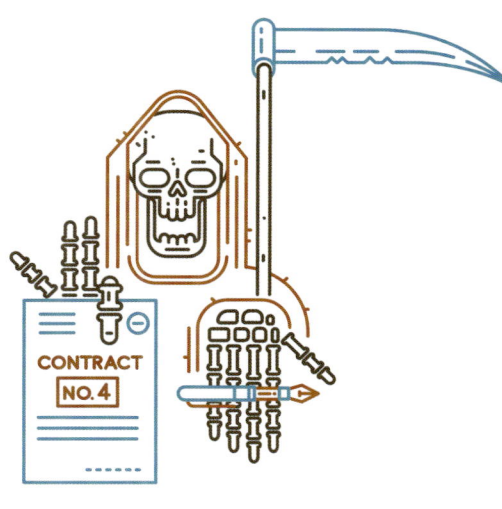
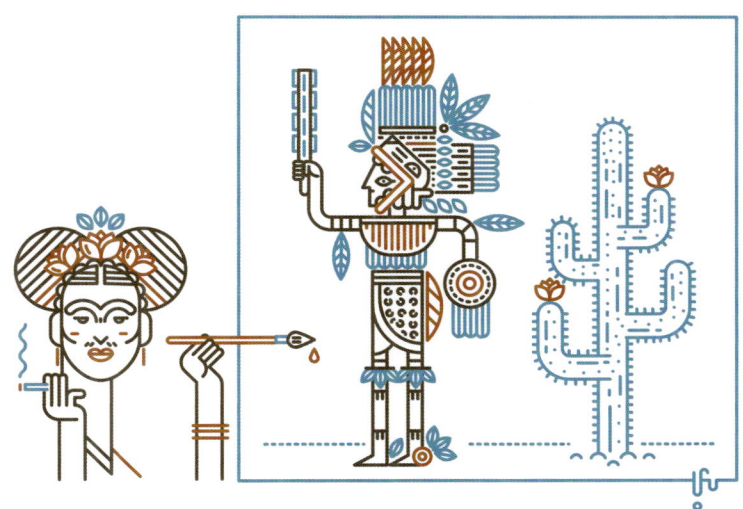

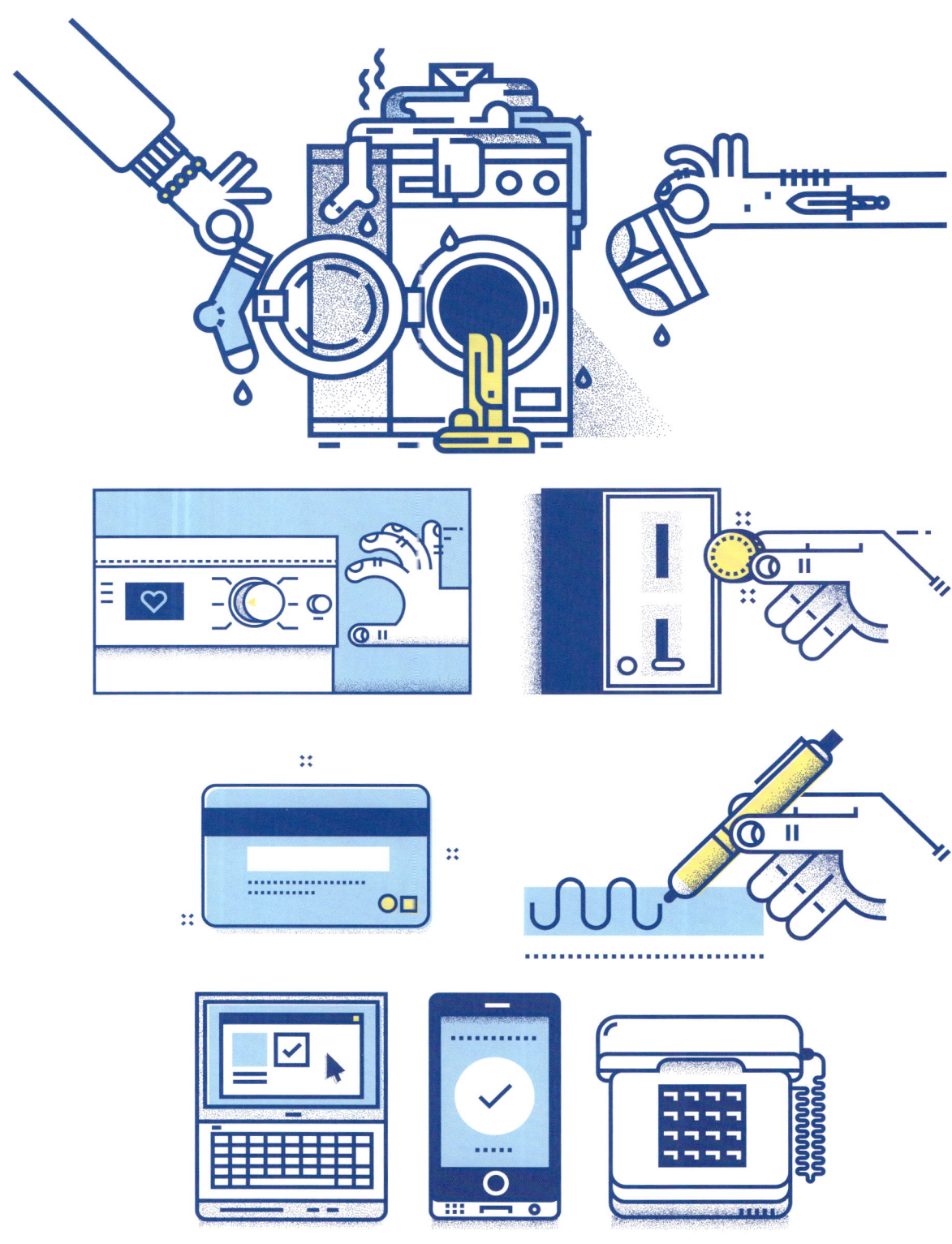

WeWash. Shine Bright.

WeWash is the Smart Home solution for doing laundry. Reserve communal machines, be informed once your laundry is done and pay with ease. All via app, website or telephone. Together with Studio Heu.Land, Musclebeaver was invited to develop the illustrations and the animations for a explainer video for WeWash.

Designer: Musclebeaver
Country: Germany
Design Agency: Studio Heu.Land Brand. Design. Code
Creative Director: Volker Heuer
Client: WeWash

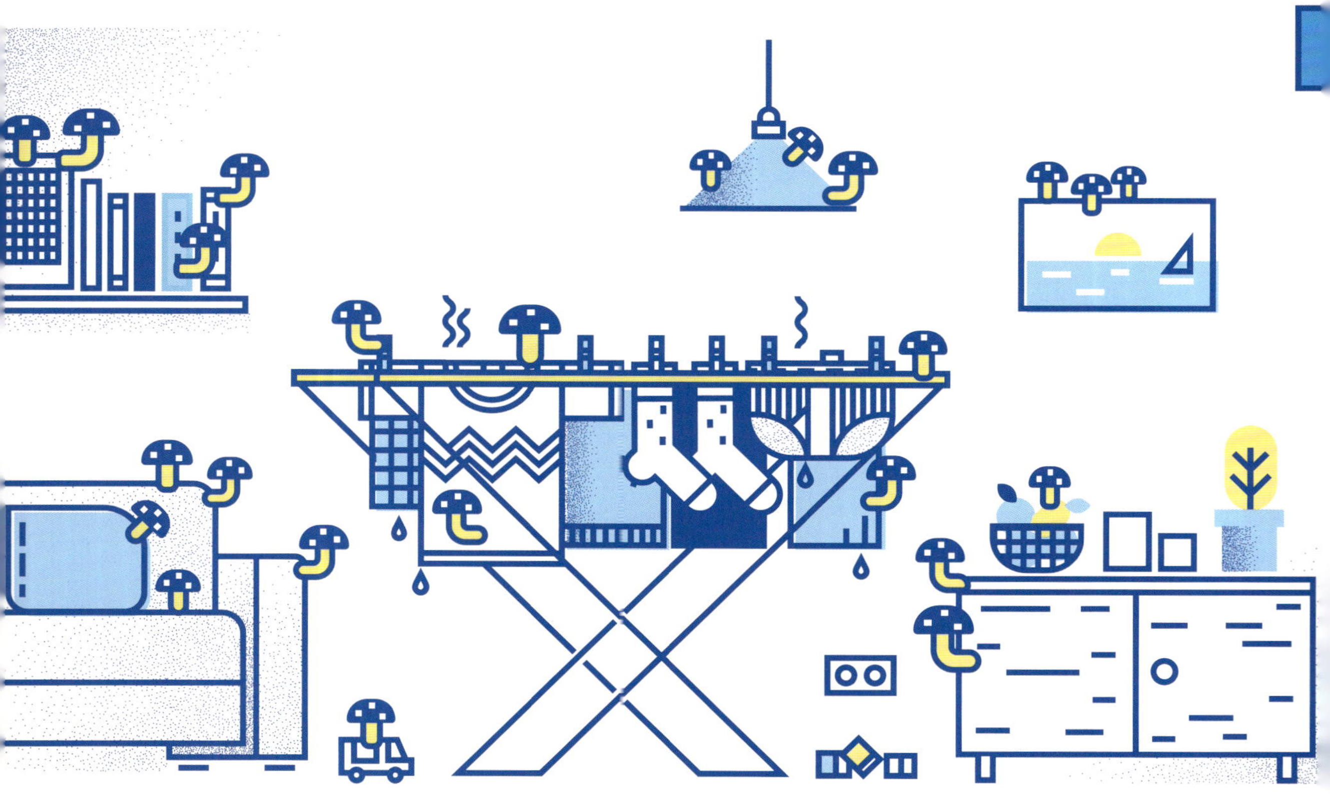

WeWash. Shine Bright.

Designer: Musclebeaver
Country: Germany

WeWash. Shine Bright.

Designer: Musclebeaver
Country: Germany

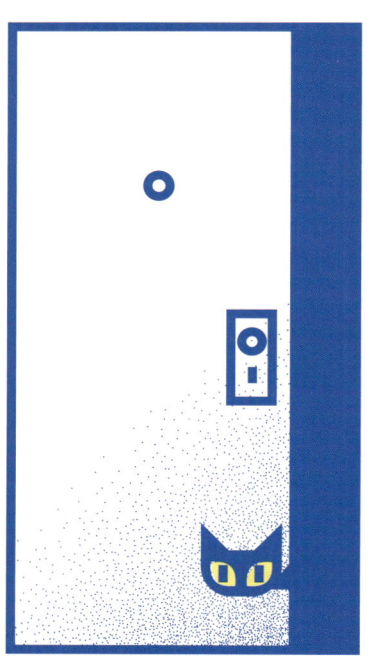

WeWash. Shine Bright.

Designer: Musclebeaver
Country: Germany

Non-Sense Project

Three posters filled with characte`s and other non-sense stuff without other ambition that play and have fun.

Designer: Enisaurus
Country: Spain

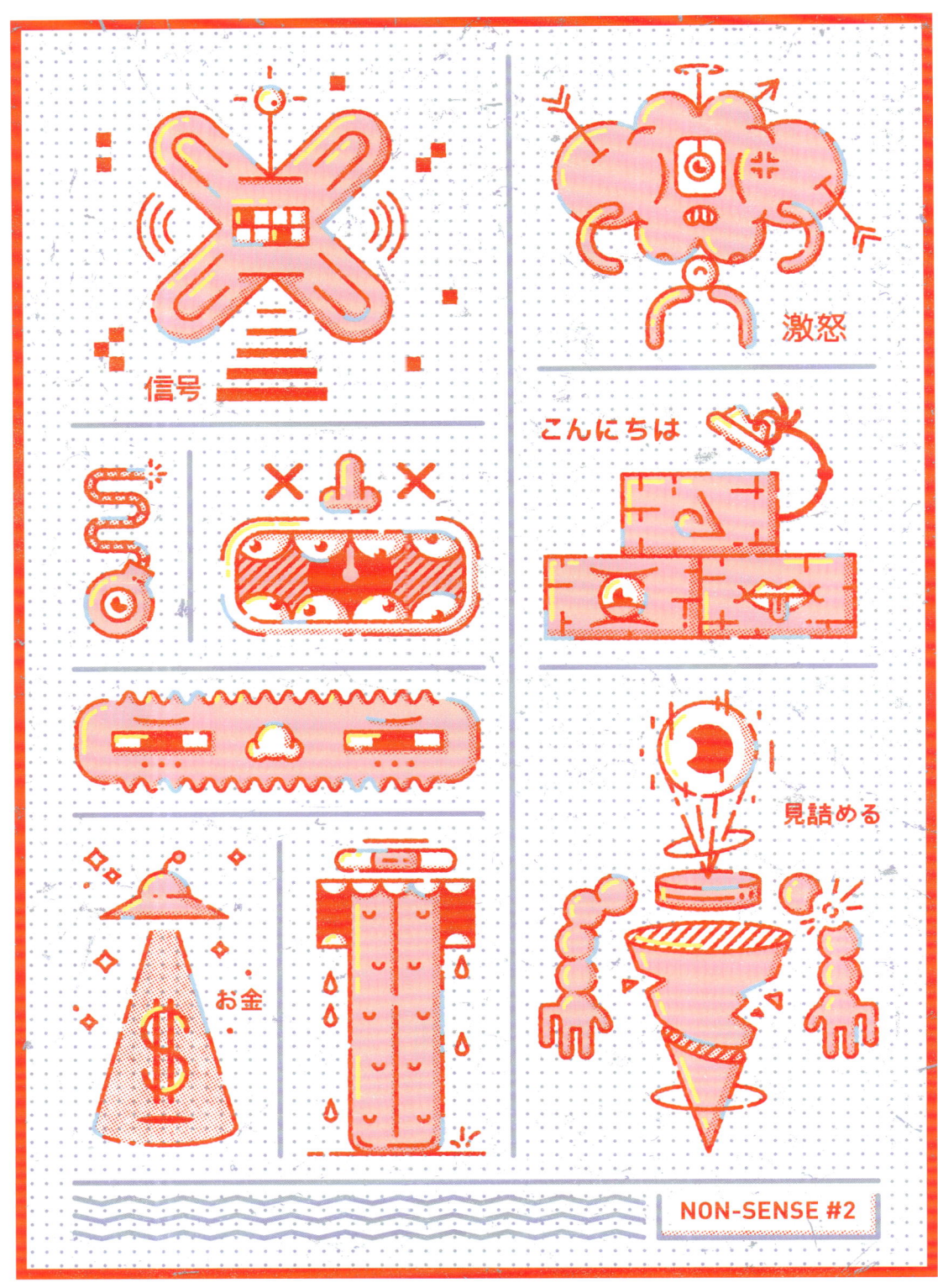

Non-Sense Project

Designer: Enisaurus
Country: Spain

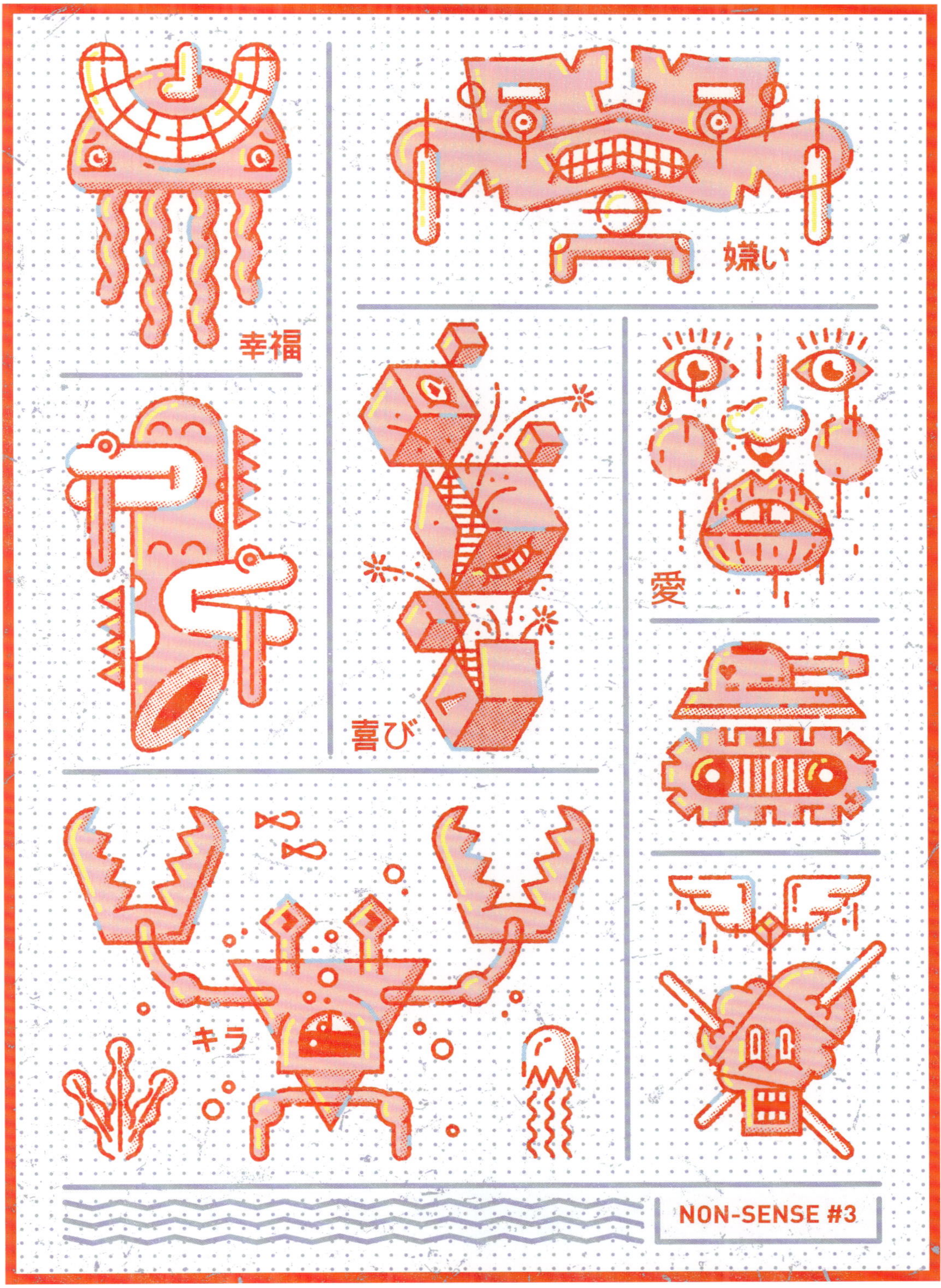

Hidden Numbers

This year Enisaurus had the privilege to be contacted by the team of 36 Days Of Type to be featured as an invited artist for developing the number 6 of the 2017's series, which also was part of the recent official exhibition in Barcelona.
He always tries to make something different that He is used to doing in his daily work, using the contest as an excuse for reaching other levels of experimentation.
The thing is that he was so motivated with the result of the number 6 that he took the decision to start working on the remaining nine numbers for getting the full collection done.
The idea was to do little individual illustrations (more than 200!) as pieces of a puzzle to build the shape of each number, playing with colors and bold lines.

Designer: Enisaurus
Country: Spain

Rectangular Patterns

Experimentation with rectangular patterns about different topics .

Designer: Enisaurus
Country: Spain

Framed Stories

This is a set composed by four short stories about different topics which Enisaurus made for fun and experimentation. He has always liked to tell something with his works and he had the idea to do it working on it like a comic sheet, using vignettes. Showing you just six frames to build the story.

City Postcards

Enisaurus created these postcards featuring five amazing cities of the world he's visited (Except Tokyo... He can't wait to visit that marvellous and beautiful place). He has alwcys liked to draw buildings since he was a child, experimenting with its geometry.

Designer: Enisaurus
Country: Spain

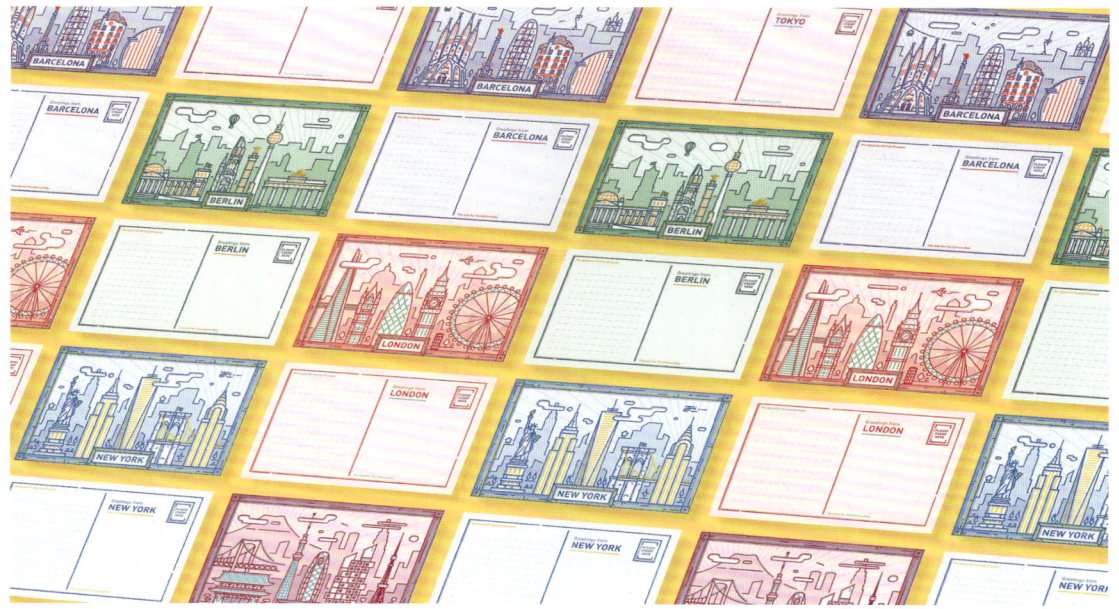

NeverFade - Guardian Angel

Designer: Hei lichee
Country: China

Picture Book "NeverFade - the Son of Winter"

Designer: Hei lichee
Country: China

241

Frog Knignt

Designer: Hei lichee
Country: China

Bee

Butterfly

Dragonfly

Unicorn

Designer: Hei lichee
Country: China

Flamingo

Bird

Designer: Hei lichee
Country: China

Penguin

Whale

Deer

Designer: Hei lichee
Country: China

Universe

Designer: Hei lichee
Country: China

Chewing Art Gallery

Desgner: Lantos Studio
Country: China
Design Agency: Lantos Studio
Photographer: Lantos Studio

NATHALIE DU PASQUIER

Claude Monet
1840–1926

Chewing Art Gallery

Desginer: Lantos Studio
Country: China

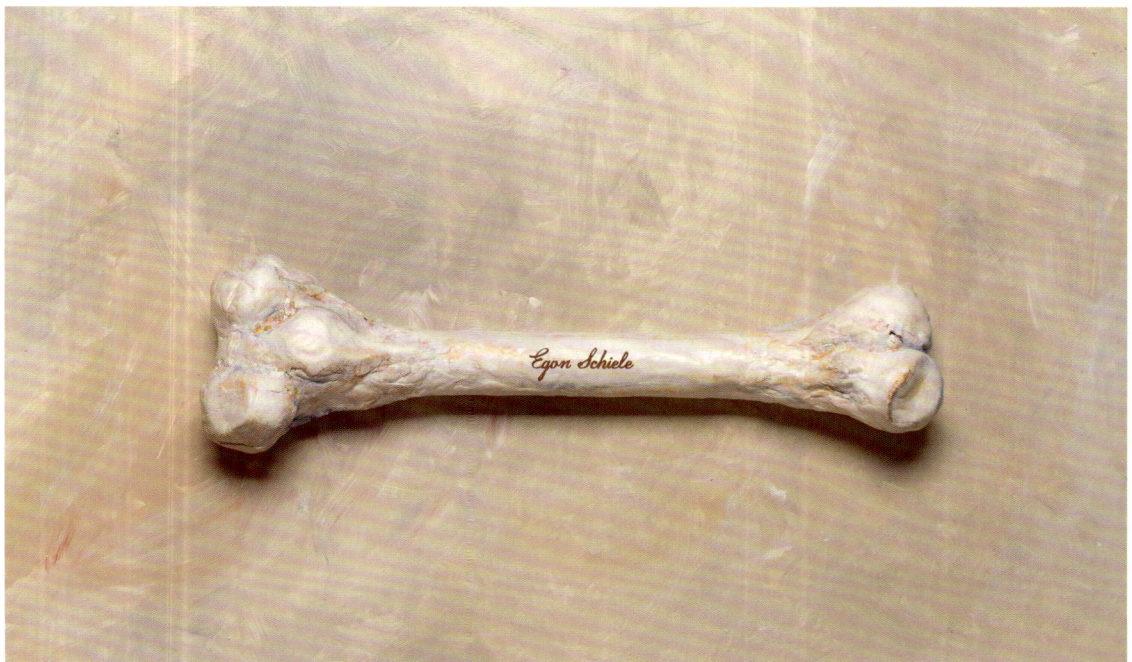

255

Chewing Art Gallery

Desgner: Lantos Studio
Country: China

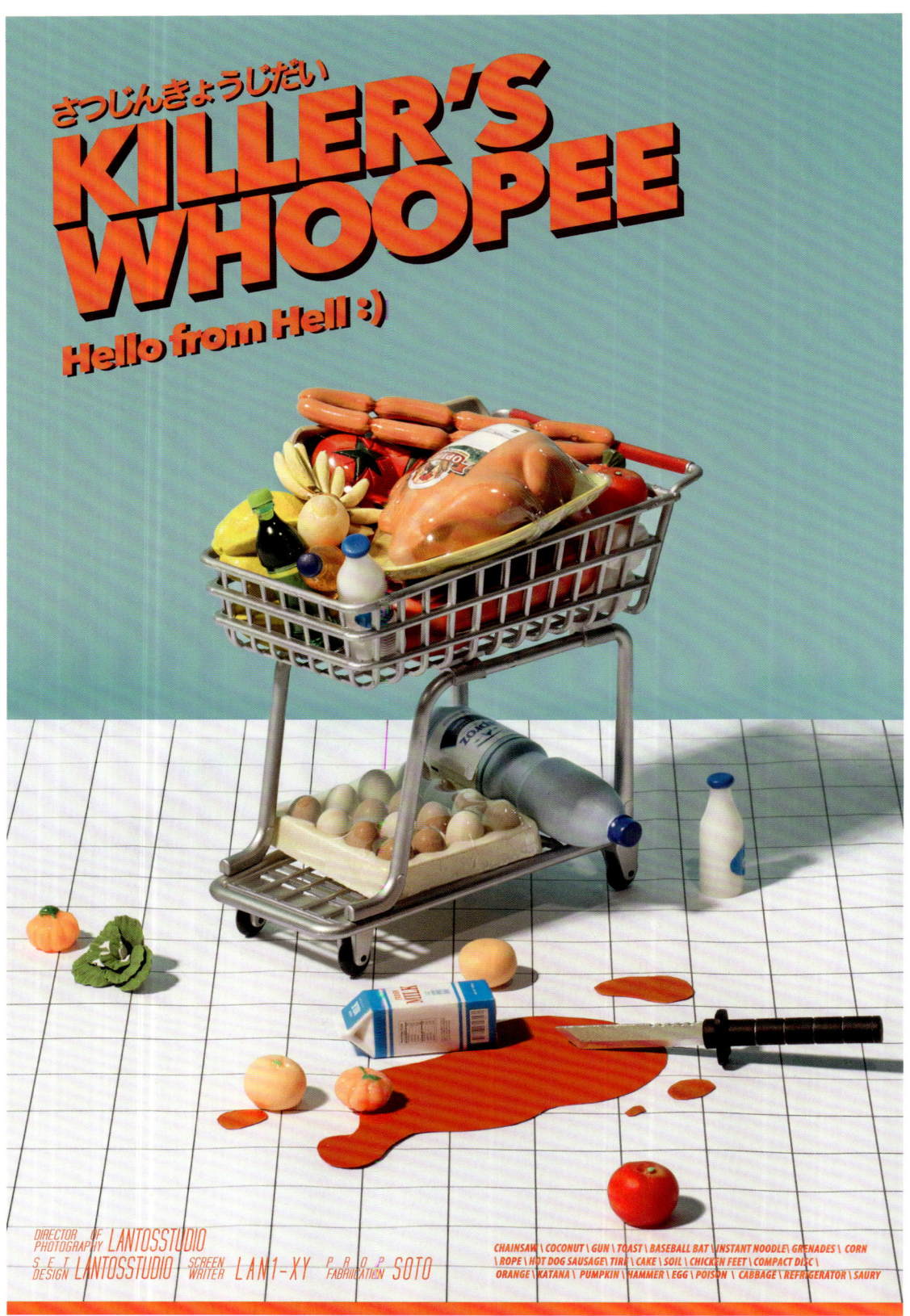

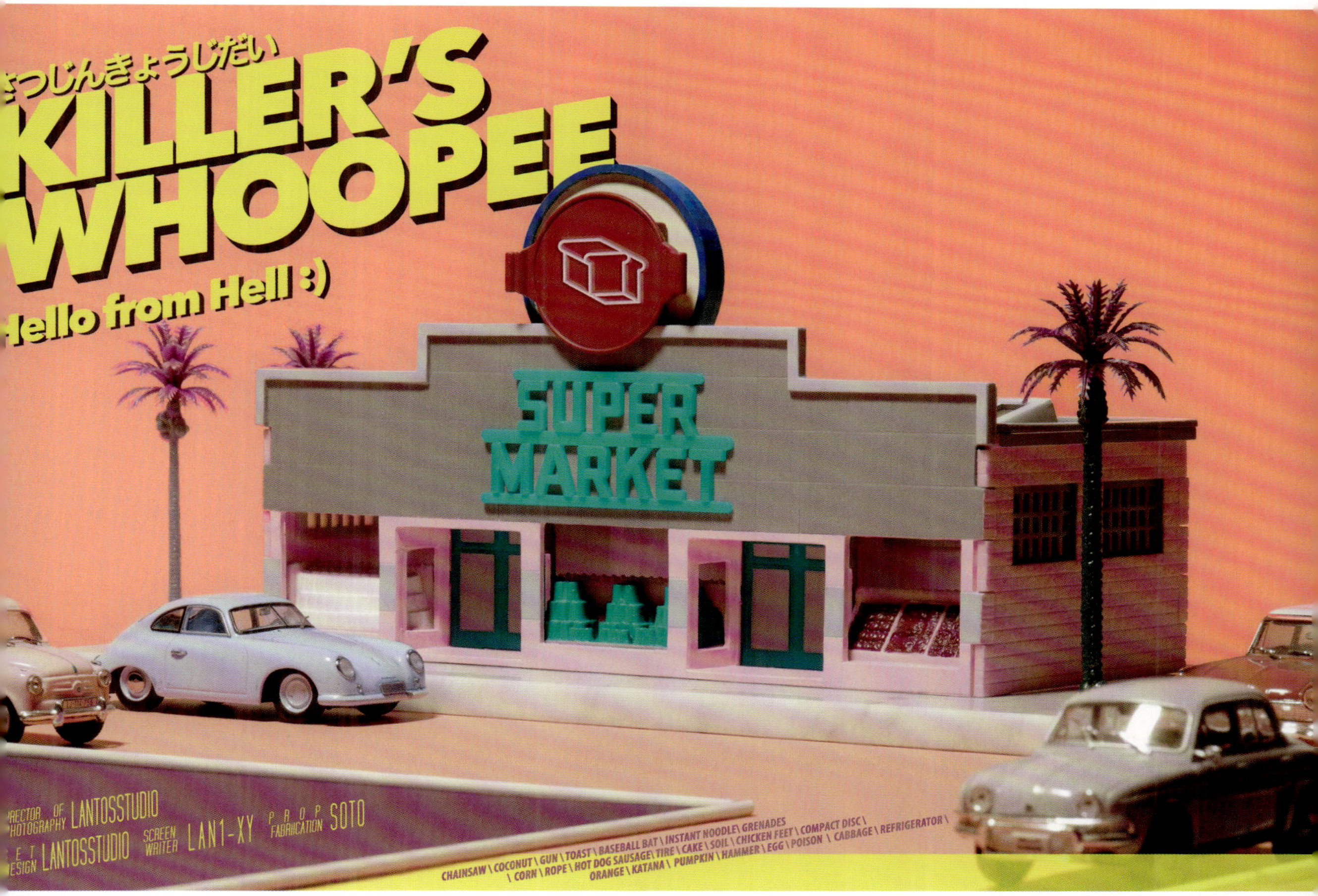

KILLER'S WHOOPEE

Desgner: Lantos Studio
Country: China
Design Agency: Lantos Studio
Photographer: Lantos Studio

YELLOW

The Yellow Feast Table

Desgner: Lantos Studio
Country: China
Design Agency: Lantos Studio
Photographer: Lantos Studio

The Green Feast Table

Desgner: Lantos Studio
Country: China
Design Agency: Lantos Studio
Photographer: Lantos Studio

The Green Feast Table

Desgner: Lantos Studio
Country: China

OLYMPIC VILLAGE MAP
奧運村地圖

Olympic Village Map

Desgner: Lantos Studio
Country: China
Design Agency: Lantos Studio
Photographer: Lantos Studio

Olympic Village Map

Desgner: Lantos Studio
Country: China

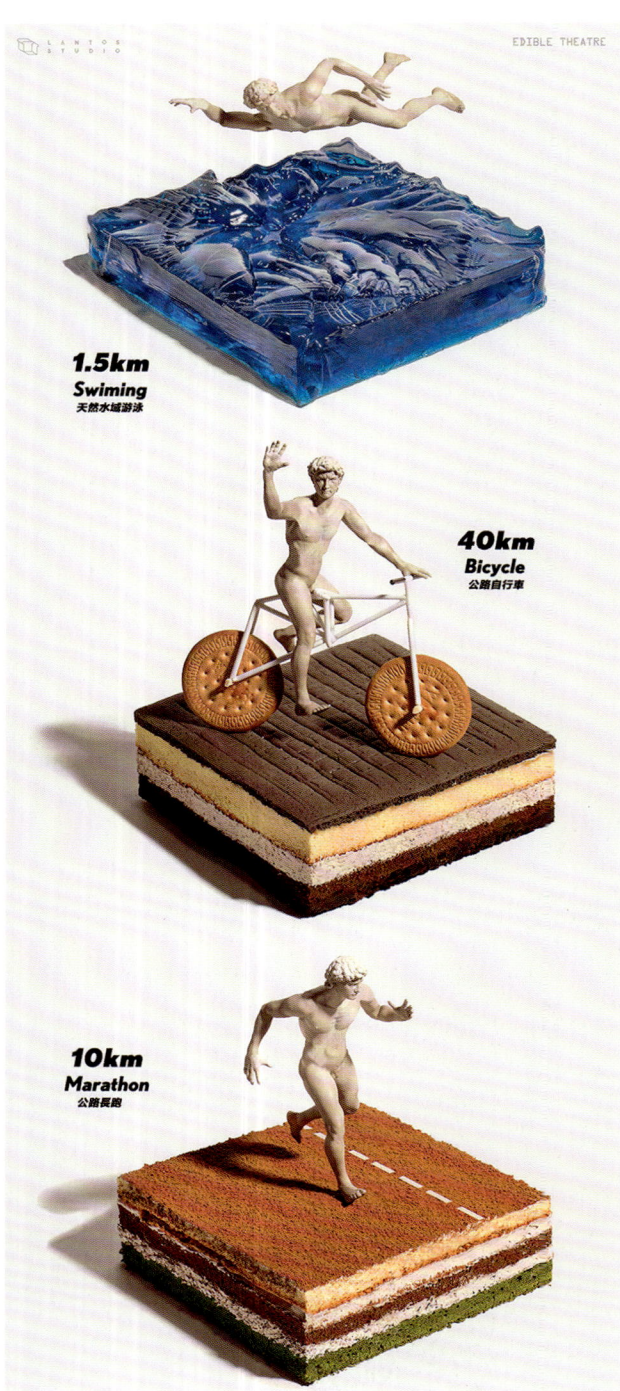

Olympic Village Map

Desgner: Lantos Studio
Country: China

2017 Astronaut Disry

Desgner: Lantos Studio
Country: China
Design Agency: Lantos Studio
Photographer: Lantos Studio

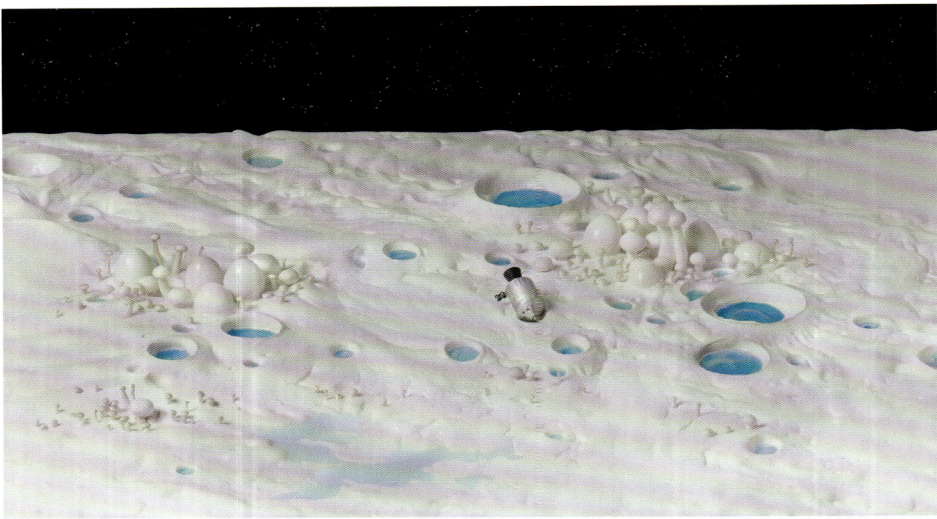

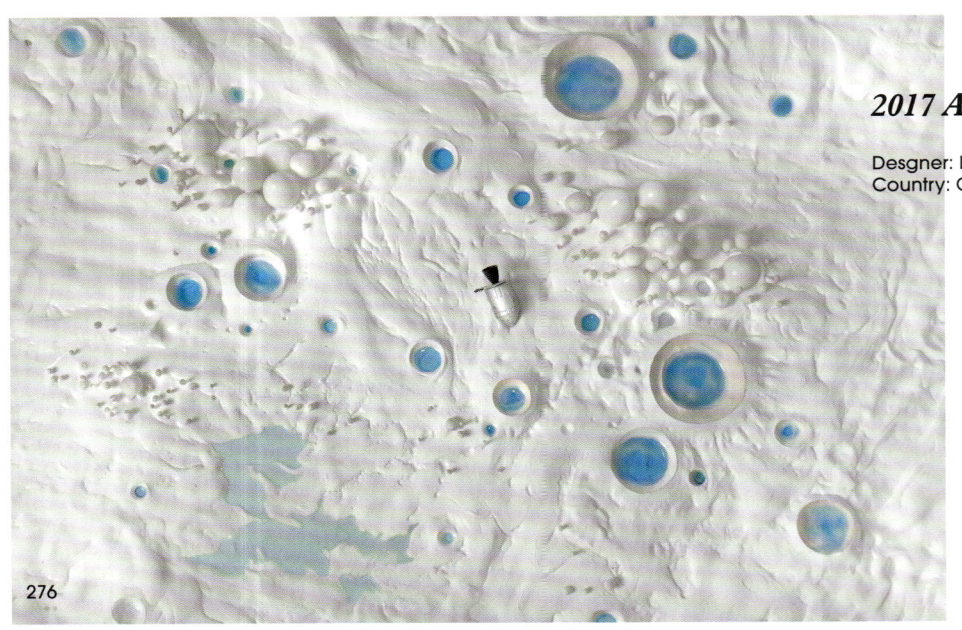

2017 Astronaut Disry

Desgner: Lantos Studio
Country: China

277

2017 Astronaut Disry

Desgner: Lantos Studio
Country: China

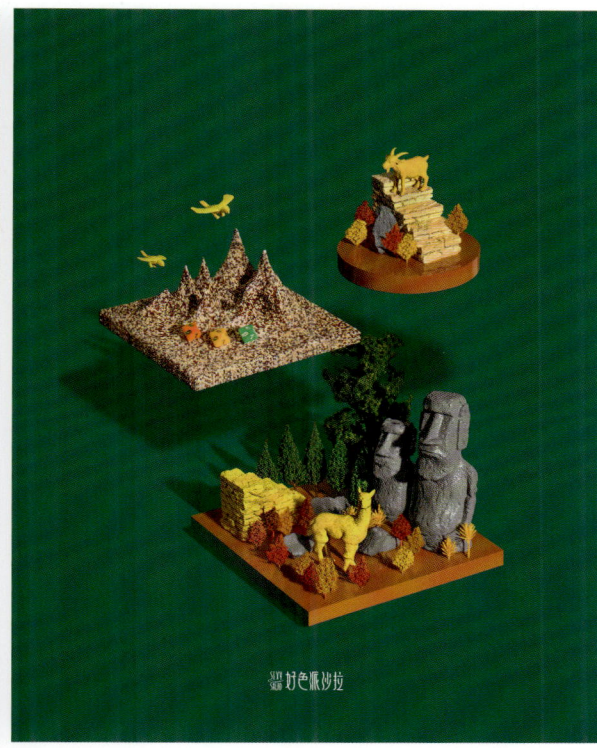

Sexy Salad

Desgner: Lantos Studio
Country: China
Design Agency: Lantos Studio
Photographer: Lantos Studio

Sexy Salad

Desgner: Lantos Studio
Country: China

Sexy Salad

Desgner: Lantos Studio
Country: China

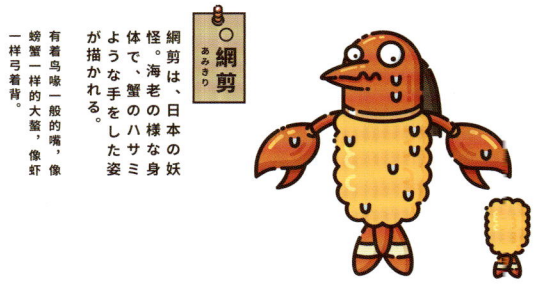

○網剪（あみきり）

網剪は、日本の妖怪で、海老の様な身体で、蟹のハサミのような手が描かれる。

網剪是一种日本的妖怪。有着鸟喙一般的嘴，螃蟹一般的大螯，像虾一样弓着背。

○猫また（ねこまた）

猫または、ネコの妖怪。

猫又是一种有着两条尾巴的猫妖，能直立行走还能够化为人形。

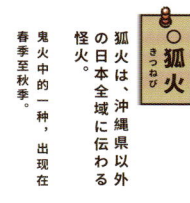

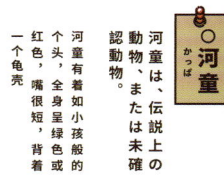

○狐火（きつねび）

狐火は、沖縄県以外の日本全域に伝わる怪火。

鬼火中的一种，出现在春季至秋季。

○河童（かっぱ）

河童は、伝説上の動物、または未確認動物。

河童有着如小孩般的个头，全身呈绿色或红色，嘴很短，背着一个龟壳。

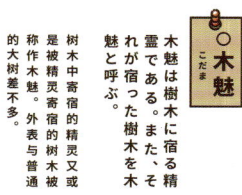

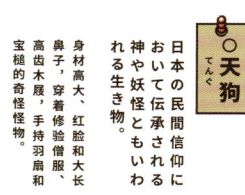

○木魅（こだま）

木魅は樹木に宿る精霊である。また、それが宿った樹木を木魅と呼ぶ。

树木中寄宿的精灵又或是被精灵寄宿的树木被称作木魅。外表与普通的大树差不多。

○天狗（てんぐ）

日本の民間信仰において伝承される神や妖怪ともいわれる生き物。

身材高大，红脸和大长鼻子，穿着修验僧服，高齿木屐，手持羽扇和宝槌的奇怪怪物。

Shin - Hyakkiyakou with Cute Style

According to Shin's panting 'Hyakkiyakou' to recreate, to make the terrified monster cute, hoping that more people can understand the monster culture.

Designer: Wenju Chen
Country: China

○火車（かしゃ）

火車は、猫の妖怪とされることが多く。

正体是猫的妖怪，会在葬礼的时候抢夺罪人的尸体。

○ふらり火（ふらりび）

ふらり火は、犬のような顔をした鳥が炎に包まれた姿で描かれている。

脸长得像狗的鸟，身体被火焰包围。

○鳴屋（やなり）

鳴屋は、家や家具が理由もなく揺れ出す現象。

寄生在家中的小妖怪，使家里的地板发出"嘎吱嘎吱"的声音。

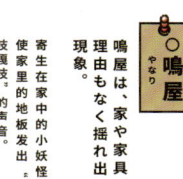

○姥が火（うばがひ）

姥ヶ火は、老女が灯油を盗み、老婆となったのだという。

偷盗神社灯油的老奶奶变成的怪火，会四处飞来飞去。

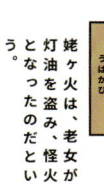

○飛頭蛮（ろくろくび）

飛頭蛮は、首が伸びるものと、首が抜け頭部が飛行するものの二種が存在する。

分为两种，一种是脖子可以伸长，一种是头可以离开身体飞行。

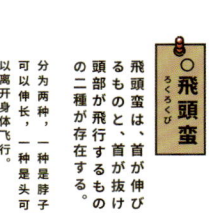

○飛頭蛮（ろくろくび）

飛頭蛮は、首が伸びるものと、首が抜け頭部が飛行するものの二種が存在する。

分为两种，一种是脖子可以伸长，一种是头可以离开身体飞行。

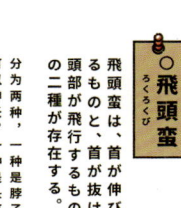

絡新婦は、美しい女の姿に化けることが出来るとされている。

絡新婦，会变为美丽的女子来诱惑男人，最后再将其杀害。

入内雀とは、人々を京に帰りたい一心の実方の怨念が雀と化した雀である。

想回归京都的藤原实方的怨念，化为鸟雀。会将农作物吃个精光。

黒塚は、鬼婆の墓、及びその鬼婆の伝説。

一种老婆婆的妖怪，会吃人，也有说法是黑塚指的是埋葬鬼婆的墓地。

玉藻前とは、鳥羽上皇の寵姫であったとされる伝説上の人物。妖狐の化身であり、正体を見破られた後殺生石になったという。

和酒吞童子一样是"日本三大邪恶妖怪"中的一个。变化为人型之时是绝世的美女。

Shin - Hyakkiyakou with Cute Style

Designer: Wenju Chen
Country: China

○倩兮女（けらけらおんな）

倩兮女は、塀越しに口をひらいて笑う巨大な女性である。

身着和服，在墙的背后出现的巨大女性。会一直咯咯的笑，以此来吓人。

○燈台鬼（とうだいき）

燈台鬼は、唐人風の衣装に身を包んだ者が、名前の通り火の灯った燭台を頭の上に乗せている。正体は人間である。

出使大唐的日本大臣被毒成了哑巴，头顶大蜡烛，成了活人灯台。

○煙々羅（えんえんら）

煙々羅は、かまどや風呂場から立ち上った煙の中に、人のような顔の形で浮かび上がるものである。

寄宿在烟中的精灵，会出现在灶台和浴室等地方，呈烟雾状，有人一样的脸。

○泥田坊（どろたぼう）

泥田坊は、見た通りの田んぼに現れる妖怪、顔が片目のみで手の指が三本しかない。

由于孩子不成器，死去的农民变成了妖怪，会出现在田里，只有一只眼睛。

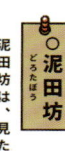

○山姥（やまうば）

山姥は、奥山に棲む老女の怪、人を食らうと考えられている。

山中的鬼婆，会吃人，又或是侍奉山神的巫女妖怪化后形成的妖怪。

○紅葉狩（もみじがり）

紅葉狩は、戸隠山に鬼がおり、平維茂によってそれが退治されたというのが共通する伝説の要素である。その鬼は女性であり、名前を紅葉である。

红叶本名吴叶，正体是第六天魔王，是一位蛇蝎美人。收到追放后，带领一群人头戴鬼面，烧杀抢劫。

○犬神白児（いぬがみしらちご）

犬神は、憑き物として伝わるモノ。白児は、犬神の弟子説や、白痴病の子供説である。

犬神的灵魂会附在人的身上，是一种被禁止的巫术。白儿是服侍犬神外貌像儿童的妖怪。

○朧車（おぼぐるま）

朧車は、半透明の牛車の前面に、本来なら簾がかかっている場所に巨大な顔がある。

牛车的前面，本来应该是挂帘子的地方，却有一张巨大的女性的脸。据说是落魄的贵族的怨恨所化。

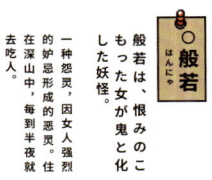

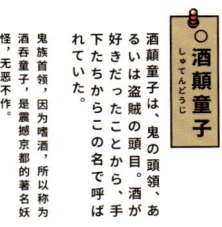

○ 般若
はんにゃ

般若は、恨みのこもった女が鬼と化した妖怪。

一种怨灵，因女人强烈的妒恶形成的恶灵。住在深山中，每到半夜就去吃人。

○ 酒顛童子
しゅてんどうじ

酒顛童子は、鬼の頭領、あるいは盗賊の頭目。酒が好きだったことから、手下たちからこの名で呼ばれていた。

酒顛童子是鬼族首领，因为嗜酒，所以称为酒吞童子，是震撼京都的著名妖怪，无恶不作。

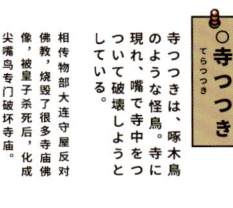

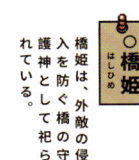

○ 寺つつき
てらつつき

寺つつきは、啄木鳥のような怪鳥。寺に現れ、嘴で寺中をつついて破壊しようとしている。

相传物部大连守屋反对佛教，烧毁了很多寺庙佛像，被皇子杀死后，化成尖嘴鸟专门破坏寺庙。

○ 橋姫
はしひめ

橋姫は、外敵の侵入を防ぐ橋の守護神として祀られている。

出现在桥边的女妖，神祇，属于日本水妖和水神。

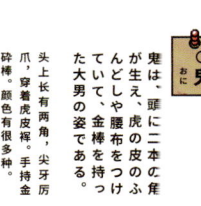
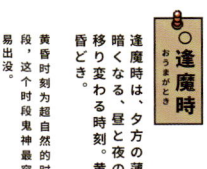

○ 鬼
おに

鬼は、頭に二本の角が生え、虎の皮のふんどしや腰布をつけていて、金棒を持った大男の姿である。

头上长有两角，尖牙厉爪，穿着虎皮挥爪，手持金砸棒。颜色有很多种。

○ 逢魔時
おうまがとき

逢魔時は、夕方の薄暗くなる、昼と夜の移り変わる時刻。黄昏どき。

黄昏时刻为超自然的时段，这个时段鬼神最容易出没。

Shin - Hyakkiyakou with Cute Style

Designer: Wenju Chen
Country: China

○ わいら
わいら

わいらは、巨大な体に、前足には太く鋭いカギ爪を1本ずつ生えた姿で描かれている。

正体不明，有着狮子和熊一样的身姫，手足都各有一个爪子，有一对翅膀。

○元興寺
（がごぜ）

元興寺は、元興寺の鬼と呼ばれる。

隐藏在寺院屋顶上的吃人妖怪。差点被一个有神力的童子抓住，逃跑时被抓去一撮毛发。

○おとろし
（おとろし）

おとろしは、長い髪におおわれ、顔に前髪をたらした姿で描かれている。

住在被人们遗忘的神社，会突然跳下来吓人，脸和身体是红的，而且有一对大牙。

○苧うに
（おうに）

苧うには、口が耳まで裂けた鬼女のような顔をした妖怪で、全身が毛に覆われている。

嘴巴一直开裂到耳朵，全身被毛覆盖。据说是山姥的一种，会用大麻帮助人们编编子。

○塗仏
（ぬりぼとけ）

塗仏とは、体の黒い坊主の妖怪で、両目玉が飛び出して垂れ下がった姿で描かれている。

生前是个修士，经常把自己的身体涂成黑色，两个眼珠是掉出来的。背上有像鱼尾巴一样的东西。

○ひょうすべ
（ひょうすべ）

ひょうすべは、ハゲ頭の人間の顔で身体がサルのような妖怪です。

起源比河童更早，是个秃头，身上有毛。

○見越
（みこし）

見越は、僧の姿で突然現れ、見上げれば見上げるほど大きくなる。

走在路上或山路里突然跳出来吓人的巨大妖怪。

○しょうけら
（しょうけら）

しょうけらは、人家の天窓から屋内を覗き込む鬼のような姿で描かれている。

常出现在古屋的屋顶，使屋中的人生病，加害那些不睡觉的人。

○宝船
たからぶね

宝船は、七福神が乗る宝物を積み込んだ帆船。宝船には珊瑚、金銀、宝石など、様々な宝物が積み込まれているという。

七福神乘坐的船，上面载有很多多金银财宝、珊瑚等等。

○人面樹
にんめんじ

人面樹は、山谷にあり、人の首のような花を咲かせた木が描かれている。

在山谷中，树的枝头上开的不是花朵而是人脸，但是不会说话。

○塵塚怪王
ちりづかかいおう

塵塚怪王は、ごみの付喪神たちの王である。

灰尘积的太多就会变成妖怪，它是其中最厉害的。头戴冠冕，穿着兽皮裙。会带领妖怪搜唐柜。

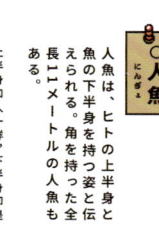

○人魚
にんぎょ

人魚は、ヒトの上半身と魚の下半身を持つ姿と伝えられる。角を持った全長11メートルの人魚もある。

上半身和人一样，下半身却是鱼，没有角，相传曾出现过11米长的头上长角的人鱼。

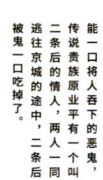
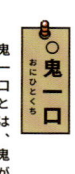

○鬼一口
おにひとくち

鬼一口とは、鬼が一口にして人間を食い殺すことをいう。

能一口将人吞下的恶鬼，传说贵族原业平有一个叫二条后的情人，两人一同逃往京城的途中，二条后被鬼一口吃掉了。

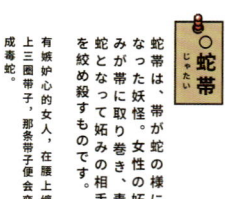

○蛇帯
じゃたい

蛇帯は、帯が蛇の様になった妖怪。女性の妬みが帯に取り巻き、毒蛇となって妬みの相手を絞め殺すものです。

有嫉妒心的女人，在腰上缠上三圈带子，那条带子便会变成毒蛇。

Shin - Hyakkiyakou with Cute Style

Designer: Wenju Chen
Country: China

○屏風覗
びょうぶのぞき

屏風覗は、屏風のぞきは、なんともいやらしい顔つきで屏風の上から覗いてくる妖怪である。

○毛羽毛現
けうけげん

毛羽毛現は、家の中のじめじめとした場所に現れるという毛むくじゃらの妖怪である。女のように毛がたくさん生えているから毛羽毛現と呼ばれるもの。

本性不明の妖怪で、全身を長い毛に覆われ、只有在头上露出两只圆圆的眼睛。

会从七尺的屏风后，窥视男女的妖怪。长着令人作呕的脸。

○狂骨
きょうこつ

狂骨は、白骨化した姿の妖怪である。井戸にうち捨てられた骸が激しい怨念によって死霊化したものとされる。

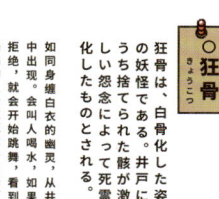

如同身缠白衣的幽灵，从井中出现。会叫人喝水，如果拒绝，就会开始跳舞，看到舞蹈的人会发狂投井自杀。

○目目連
もくもくれん

目目連は、荒れ果てた家の障子に無数の目が浮びあがった姿がある妖怪である。

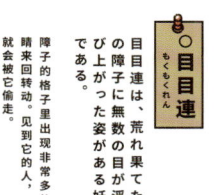

障子的格子里出现非常多的眼睛来回转动。见到它的人，眼珠就会被它偷走。

○目競
めくらべ

目競は、清盛が遭遇したという妖怪である。

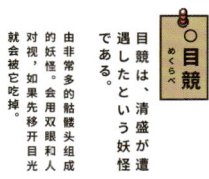

由非常多的粘髏头组成的妖怪。会用双眼和人对视，如果先移开目光就会被它吃掉。

○後神
うしろがみ

後神は、臆病神の一種であり、突然人の背後に現れ後ろ髪を引っ張る。

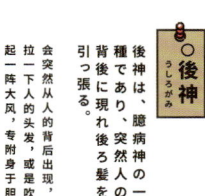

会突然从人的背后出现，拉一下人的头发，或是吹起一阵大风，专附身于胆小或优柔寡断的人。

○鵺
ぬえ

鵺は、サルの顔、タヌキの胴体、トラの手足を持ち、尾はヘビ。

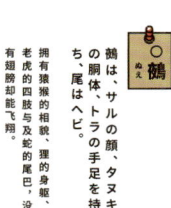

拥有猿猴的相貌、狸猫的身躯、老虎的四肢与及蛇的尾巴，没有翅膀却能飞翔。

○以津真天
いつまで

以津真天は、顔が人間のようで、体はヘビのようで、翼長は1丈の尺もあったという。

饿死的人化为的凶鸟，有人的脸和蛇的身子。会喷出火焰。

○ 乳鉢坊
にゅうばちぼう

乳鉢坊は、銅盤が変化して生まれた日本の妖怪である。銅钱变成的妖怪，邪恶的灵魂附着在葫芦上变成的妖怪。会躲在树丛中吓人。

○ 瓢箪小僧
ひょうたんこぞう

瓢箪小僧は、瓢箪が変化して生まれた日本の妖怪である。邪恶的灵魂附着在葫芦上变成的妖怪，会在树丛中吓人。

○ 骨傘
ほねからかさ

骨傘は、唐傘の付喪神化した妖怪。用了很久的油纸伞所化成的妖怪，付喪神的一种，样子像蝙蝠，龙头鱼身。

○ 木魚達磨
もくぎょだるま

木魚達磨は、だるまのようなひげの生えた顔をして円座にのっている木魚の妖怪である。木鱼上长出了达摩的脸。附在人的身上会让人失眠。

○ 鉦五郎
しょうごろう

鉦五郎は、鉦鼓が妖怪となった付喪神。「五郎」の名前は大阪の豪商で、關所となった淀屋辰五郎の名にちなむとされる。钲鼓化成的妖怪，是淀屋辰五郎制作钲鼓，辰五郎死后就附身在它上面，如果有人太自傲，钲五郎就会不敲自鸣。

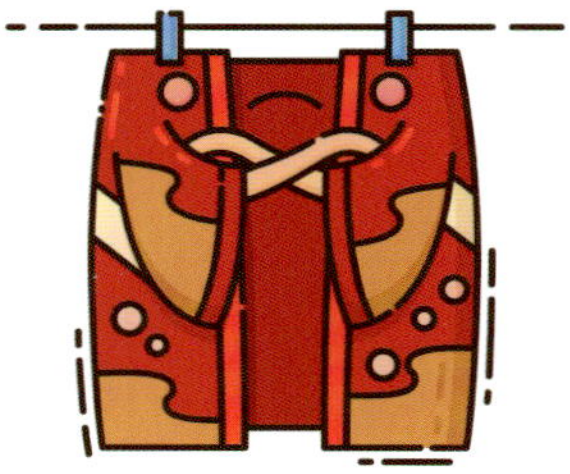

○ 小袖の手
こそでのて

小袖の手は、小袖の袖から、幽霊らしき女性の手が伸びたもの。死者生前的衣服中伸出的手，传说是女人对漂亮的衣服的执念所化。

○ 芭蕉精
ばしょうのせい

芭蕉精は、芭蕉の霊が人の姿をとるなどして人化かすというもの。琉球遍布芭蕉树，女性如果晚上六点以后在芭蕉林遇到美貌的男子，便会怀上鬼胎。只有携带刀具才可避免怪异。

○ 機尋
はたひろ

機尋は、布の妖怪。機で織られた布がヘビの姿と化したもの。女人因为埋怨外出不归的丈夫，所织的布化成了蛇，去寻找丈夫。

○ 硯の魂
すずりのたましい

硯の魂は、硯の中に海が現れ、やがて源平の合戦のような様子になったという意味である。砚中出现了源平合战的场景，可能是战场中的怨灵寄宿在砚中所造成的。

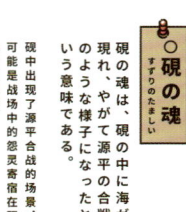

Shin - Hyakkiyakou with Cute Style

Designer: Wenju Chen
Country: China

○ 古庫裏婆（こくりばば）

古庫裏婆は、寺の庫裏に隠れ住む、死体を掘り起こして皮を剥ぎ食らったりするのだという。

隐居在寺庙仓库里的老婆婆，会挖掘尸体，将其剥皮吃掉。

○ 面霊気（めんれいき）

面霊気は、面の妖怪。優れた作品の面が古くなって魂を宿した付喪神である。

面的妖怪，优秀的能面作品，因为老旧而成为了付丧神。

○ 白粉婆（おしろいばば）

白粉婆は、ひどく腰の曲がり、大きな破れ傘を頭に被り、右手で杖をつき、左手には酒徳利を持っている老婆の妖怪である。

在雪天出现，弯着腰，一手拄着拐杖，一手拿着一瓶酒，会欺骗女性用白粉涂脸来获得他们的脸皮。

○ 幣六（へいろく）

幣六は、事触れの紙を振りかざし、ご神託と称してデマを流し、人々を混乱に陥れる妖怪である。

手持御币的妖怪哦，会假传神旨，给人带来混乱。

○ 古空穂（ふるうつぼ）

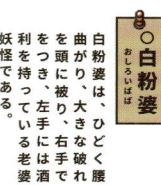

古空穂は、歳月を経たことでかつての武功や栄光が忘れられた靱が付喪神になったという。

曾经立下战功的箭袋，历经长年累月被人遗忘后，变成的妖怪。

○ 髪鬼（かみおに）

髪鬼は、人間の女性の怨みの念や嫉妬心が自分の頭髪にこもって妖怪と化したものとされる。

女性因怨念和嫉妒心变成的妖怪。就算剪了，还是会无限的生长。

○ 無垢行縢（むくむかばき）

無垢行縢は、怨念を持った、行縢の妖怪である。

因为主人被人杀害，满怀怨念的行縢变成的妖怪，势必要为主人报仇。

○ 角盥漱（つのはんぞう）

角盥漱は、平安時代の小野小町の使用していた角盥漱の妖怪として創作されたものである。

和歌诗人小町所用的角盥漱变成的妖怪。头部是个角盥漱，长着鬼角。

Eating, Drinking, Spending

Designer: Wenju Chen
Country: China

◆ YOUQIANHUA ◆

The Werewolves of Miller's Hollow

Designer: Wenju Chen
Country: China

Maomao Cat Project

Maomao Cat was a cartoon character created by Ge Yin in 2003 and was registered in 2009. Nearly ten works have been published. There is a certain philosophy in Maomao Cat's cartoon humor. There is some truth in making people laugh.

Designer: Yin Ge
Country: China
Design Agency: Maomao cat stdio

毛哥说我站在了一个非常非常重要的位置上

慢慢来就是最快的

旺仔 有什么伤心事啊 说出来 让我开心一下

劳动节快乐 劳动节快乐 那为什么你们劳动节不劳动

Maomao Cat Project

Designer: Yin Ge
Country: China

我们都想把麻烦推开
离自己越远越好

结果
麻烦就会
越麻烦

Maomao Cat Project

Designer: Yin Ge
Country: China

既然选了在路上
那就风雨无阻的走下去吧

Maomao Cat Project

Designer: Yin Ge
Country: China

笑对人生

人生本来一场戏
何必处处费心计
苦也经历
乐也经历
只要努力
就把苦乐当儿戏
反正最后都是回忆

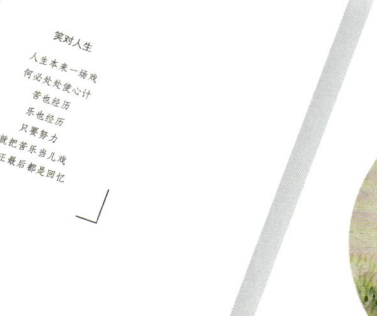

如果吼能解决问题
那驴将统治世界

问题就两种
没饭吃，饿出来的
吃饱了，撑出来的

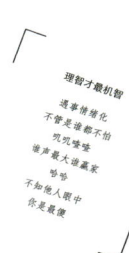

理智才最机智

遇事情绪化
不管是谁都不怕
吼吼嗒嗒
谁声最大谁赢家
爷爷
不知他人眼中
你是最傻

你要是不会玩生活
生活就把你给玩了

瞎折腾

生活一地乱麻
总想与你
时时较个高下
去吧去吧
反正不是她玩你
就是你玩她
死命折腾
灵魂才不会疲乏

月光下
，锦绣年华
事纷杂
下

你觉得你用
六位数的密码
保护着三位数的存款
有意义吗

守护

有些东西要一直守护
比如爱情
比如你的银行卡
哪怕只有三位数

311

Maomao Cat Project

Designer: Yin Ge
Country: China

Vietnamese Food Watercolor

Designer: Huynh Kim Lien
Country: Vietnam
Design Agency: Kaa illustration

Vietnamese Food Watercolor

Designer: Huynh Kim Lien
Country: Vietnam

BANH PIA

Vietnamese Food Watercolor

Designer: Huynh Kim Lien
Country: Vietnam

Hand book illustrations

Designer: Studio-Takeuma
Country: Japen

Phoenicopterus ruber
Caribbean Flamingo

Jaguar
Panthera onca
名前 あさひ
葉月旭

Elephas maximus
アジアゾウの
秋都トンカム

シロフクロウのイリーナ
Bubo scandiacus

Hand book illustrations

Designer: Studio-Takeuma
Country: Japen

No.111-11-11 Scarlet Macaw
Ara macao

メキシコ・中米からコロンビア・ブラジルなどアマゾン川流域の森林に小さな群れで生息する

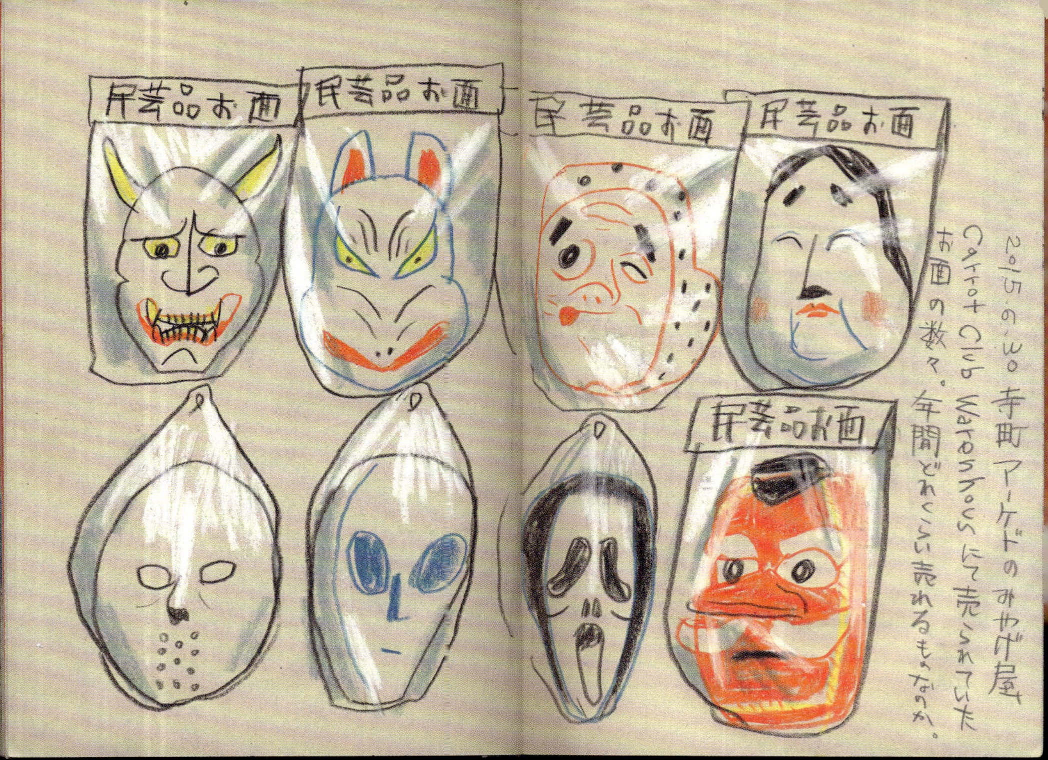

2015.6.30 寺町アーケードのみやげ屋 Carrot Club Warehouse にて売されていたお面の数々。年間どれくらい売れるものなのか。

2013.7.16 祇園祭宵山 宵山の六時になったら動かずと歩いてたオッちゃんが言ってたので そんなこんなで蟷螂 もう御輿はいいから 蟷螂を大きく描くおまけ 蟷螂山三回戦 蟷螂ちゃん 屋根はみたいな物がいた。しかしクレヨンは汚れる。

この蟷螂山、何度も火災で消失していて、1981年に修理され復活したそうです。つまり、僕と同じ年だ。

見に来たら鎌を振り上げて羽を動かしていた。からくり人形である。

町内会の人が描いたとみられる手描きの提灯に蟷螂と描いてた。漢字、蛸でも良いのかしら。

當螂山

Hand book illustrations

Designer: Studio-Takeuma
Country: Japen

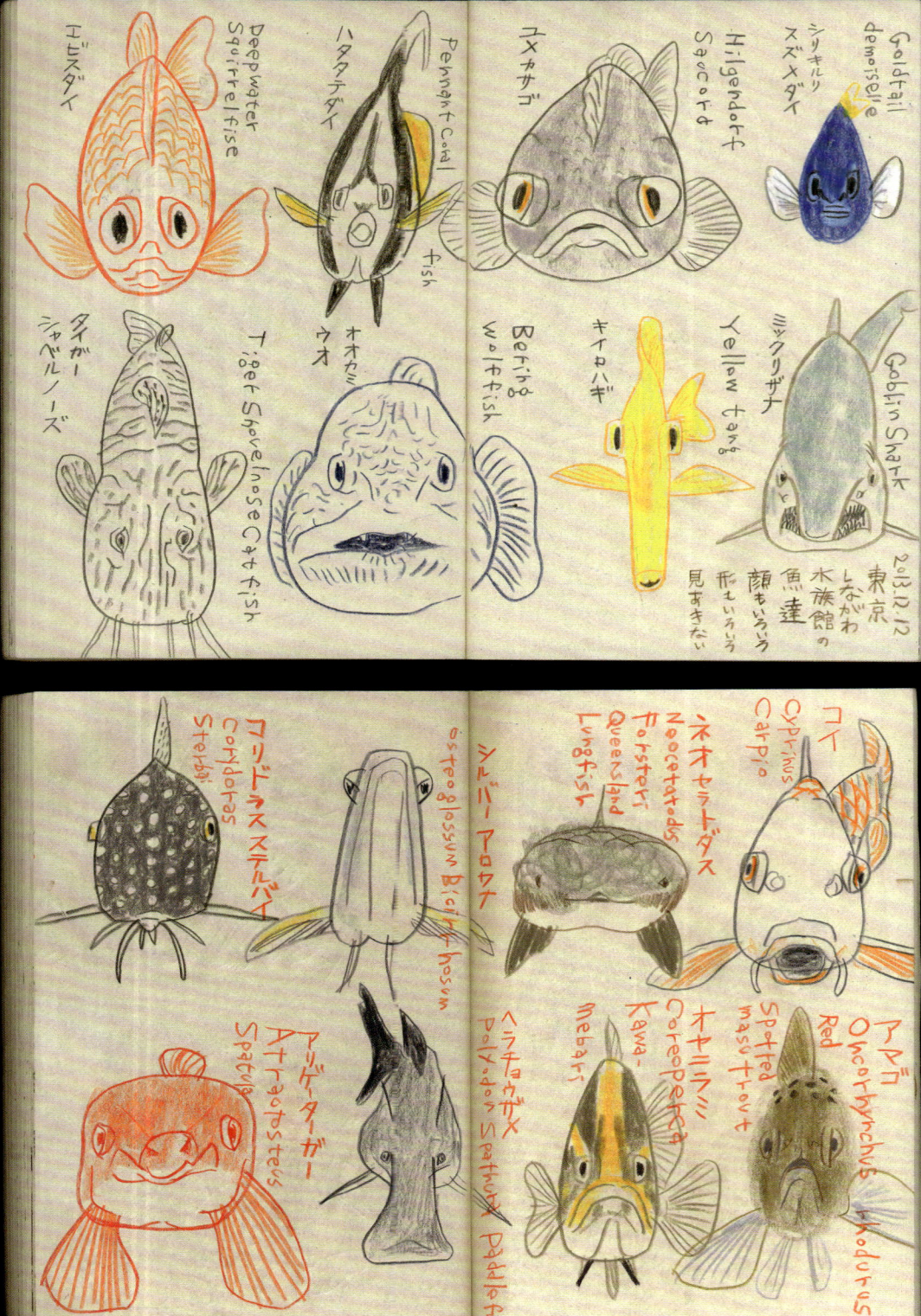

Hand book illustrations
Designer: Studio-Takeuma
Country: Japan

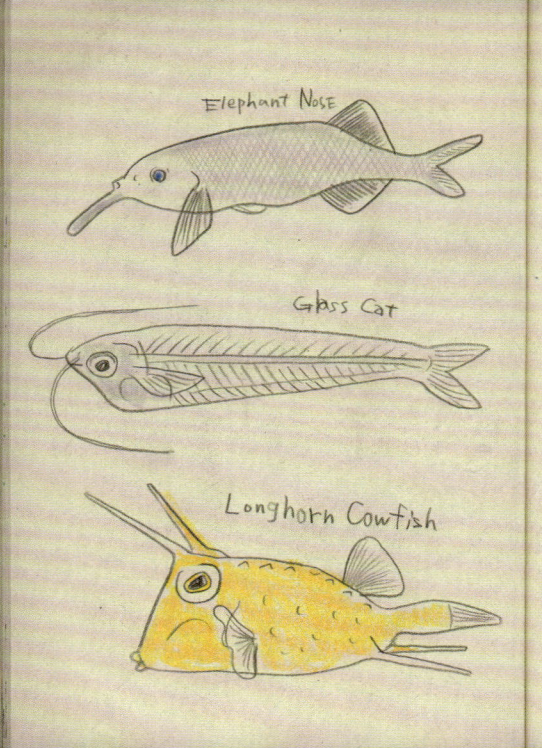

申神
安底羅大将
Andira

No.2-20 奈良国立博物館仏像館、久し振りに奈良でスケッチしました。仏像を描くのは久し振り。やはりスケッチスタート。仏像は良いですね。まずは十二の神将に。神将とは薬師如来を守護する武神です。

亥神
宮毘羅大神
Kombhira

前回来たときには展示されていなかった仏像も何体かいた。入れかわって今回なかったのもいた。

定期的に来ないとだめですね。

なお、もちろん午神もいます。今回は撮影禁止。

小面
Ko'omote

増女
Zouonna

喝食
Kasshiki

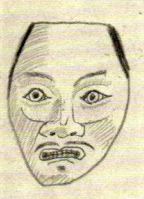
三日月
Mikazuki

呉公
Goko

酔胡王
Suiko'o

胡徳楽
Kotokuraku

崑崙八仙
Korobase

2015.8.18. 東京上野、国立科学博物館
日本館の3階の フタバスズキリュウ骨格

花屋で花を買って描く。ギャラリーくぶの絵話室の授業。水仙とか冬に咲く花ってけなげに思える。勝手な想像。

2015.2.27 花って普通の良いですわ普通のこと言ってすみません

2014.4.13 葉桜を描くのは集中力も万全の時でなければ火傷する。そんな32の春もあかん限界。いる時も素敵ですが散り出して侘びた風情になっている時も好き。もちろん桜餅も大好き。手直しの状態をみると知った。桜は咲きほこって

Hand book illustrations

Designer: Studio-Takeuma
Country: Japen

ホロホロチョウ
2016.6.26
京都市動物園にて

Guinea Fowl
Numida mereagris

ほんとは黒地に白の点々に白抜きの白の点々なんです。

傘にも色々あるけど閉じる時のねじりの向きは同じなんですな。たまたまかな。

2016.5.27

CAUDEX

TUKKA JA KUKKA
トゥッカ ヤ クッカ
※オベサとラモッシマはコーデックスで

Hand book illustrations

Designer: Studio-Takeuma
Country: Japen

Hand book illustrations

Designer: Studio-Takeuma
Country: Japen

whale shark
ジンベイザメ
大きいと言いたい為の見開きぶち抜き。

2013.3.15
海遊館

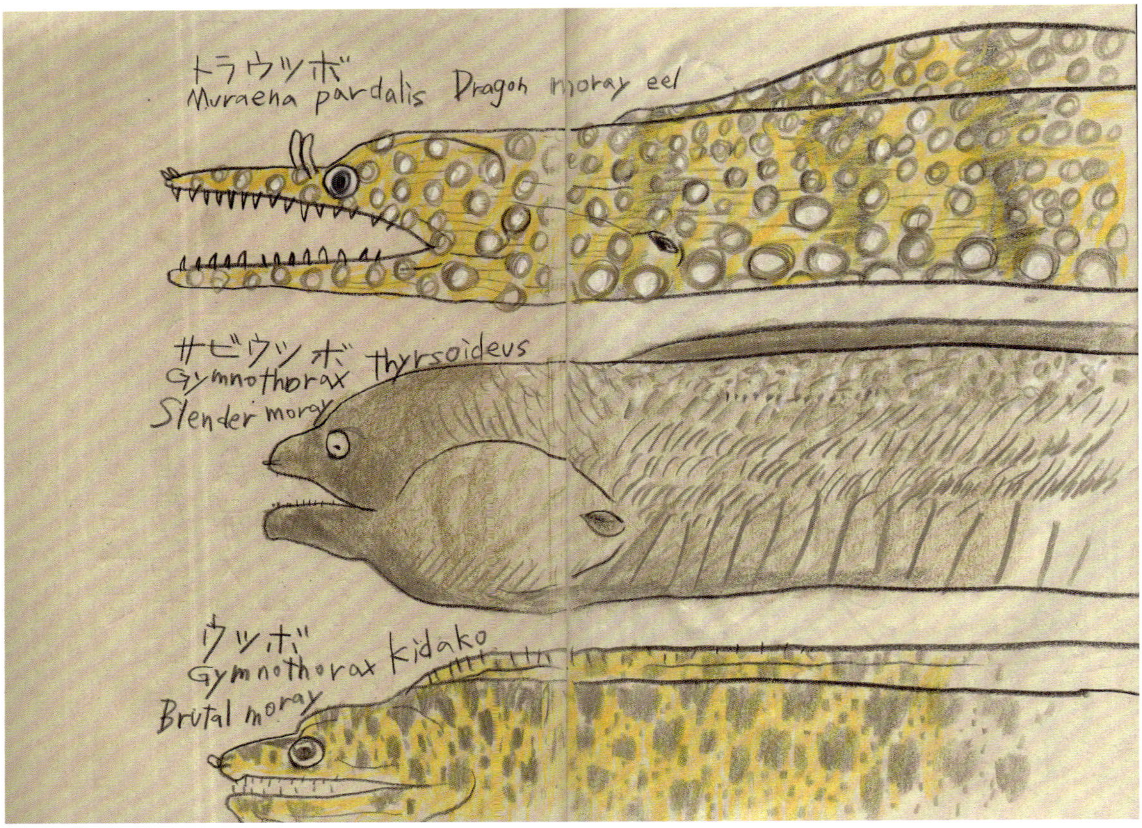

トラウツボ
Muraena pardalis Dragon moray eel

サビウツボ
Gymnothorax thyrsoideus
Slender moray

ウツボ
Gymnothorax kidako
Brutal moray

国立民族学博物館
National Museum of Ethnology

South Asia Ox figure
たぶん インド

40分ちょいと時間が かかった。これでも最速 で描いたつもりです。 こんな模様は上から 描きたせる画材で描くべきですね。

赤い色鉛筆を3本 持っていたから良かった ですが、1本なら途中 で撃沈する処でした。

2015.9.23 マンドリルのベンケイ10才 まだ若いので血気さかんらしい

Hand book illustrations
Designer: Studio-Takeuma
Country: Japen

serial work "Hedgehog's hug"

The title stands for the oxymoronic idea. These work deals with humor, black joke, nonsense and trick.

Designer: Studio-Takeuma
Country: Japen

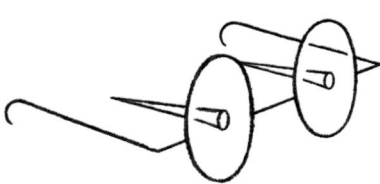

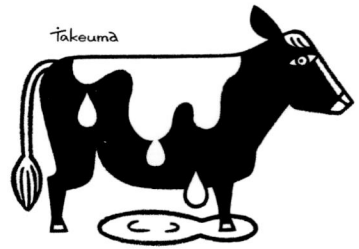

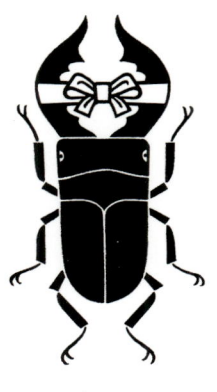

serial work "Hedgehog's hug"

Designer: Studio-Takeuma
Country: Japen

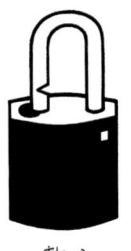

serial work "Hedgehog's hug"

Designer: Studio-Takeuma
Country: Japen

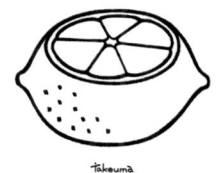

Move Font 1 Dozen

Designer: Studio-Takeuma
Country: Japen

Apple forbidden fruit

Apple discovery

Apple expert

Apple doping

alley marking   cattle mutilation   *alley catch*

Designer: Studio-Takeuma
Country: Japen

 aggression

cattle mutilation

Designer: Studio-Takeuma
Country: Japen

puddle

Designer: Studio-Takeuma
Country: Japen

Our Last Summer

bum

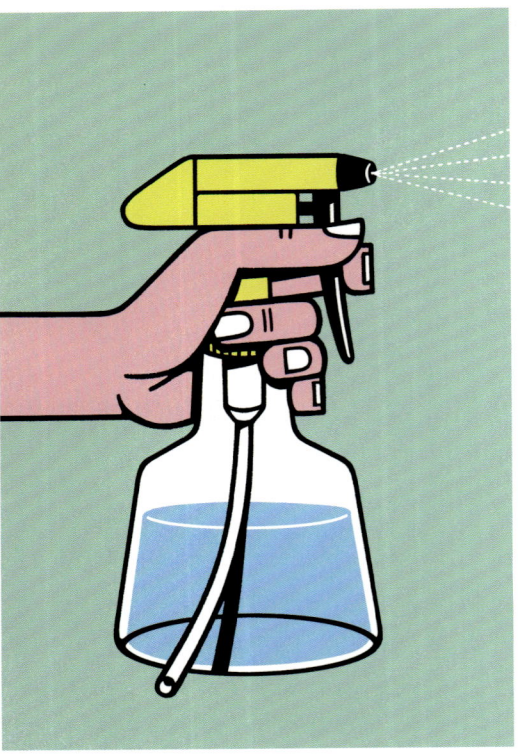

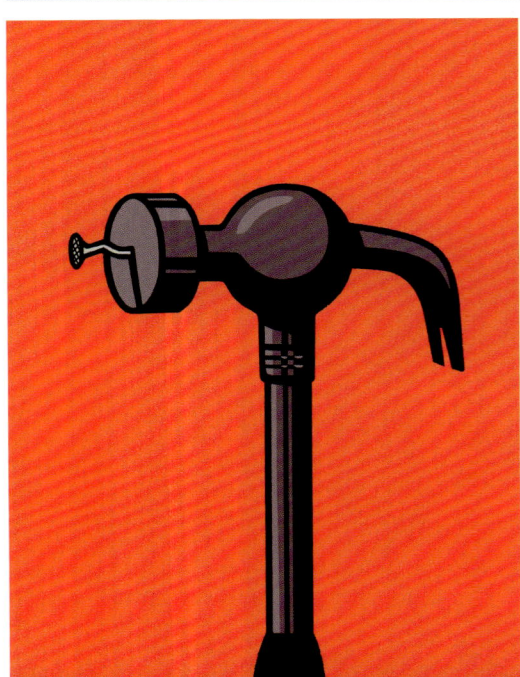

Tools

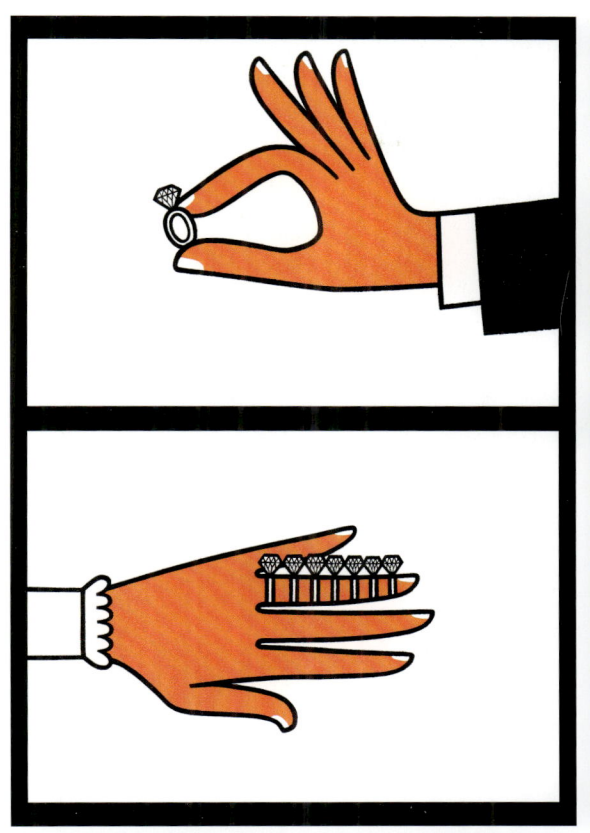
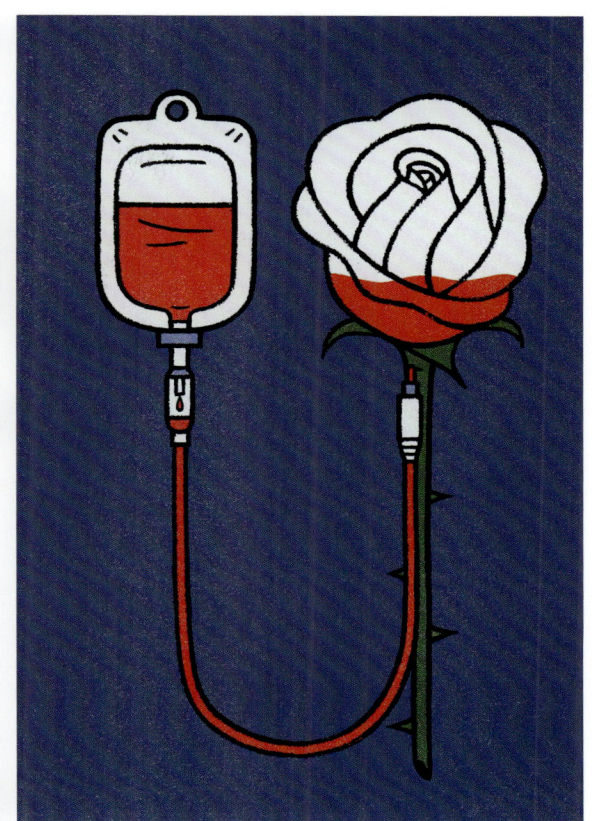

FULL HOUSE   *Red*

Corkscrew

Designer: Studio-Takeuma
Country: Japen

stuffed with straw

iron flower

Physics

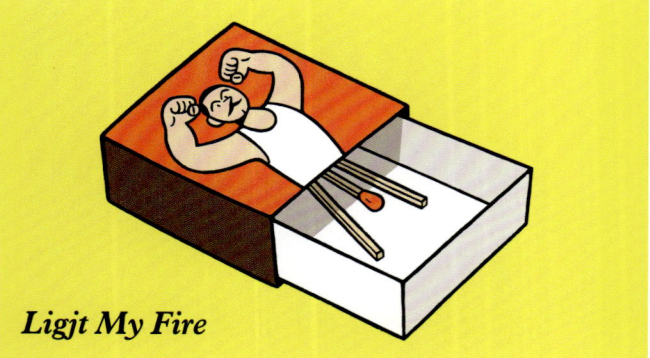

Ligjt My Fire

avocado

moon

next door

Designer: Studio-Takeuma
Country: Japen

slope

Doggy

proportion, Let's take a walk, dogging, Borzoi

Designer: Studio-Takeuma
Country: Japen

Hunter
Designer: Studio-Takeuma
Country: Japen

Bird

camouflage

decor

Designer: Studio-Takeuma
Country: Japen

Graphics can be Managed

Content

1983ASIA — China
006-075

There is an eidolon with magic strength behind everything in nature. KIDDD advocates the idea of green, natural and healthy teaching. Centered on the core idea of "there is an eidolon behind everything", the brand is designed in shape on the basis of "mountain" that produces everything and refines the cyan from nature symbolizing the flourishing vitality to imply "the pupils surpass the master". In this way, we have formed our exclusive and distinctive vision symbol. The combination of the adorable role design and a rich story-related visual system implies that every ingenious child is an adorable eidolon. They have their own pluses and minuses but with unlimited potential. In addition to the enlightenment in skill, they need to learn how to get along with others and nature in the course of studying and learn to respect and cherish others and nature as a virtue so as to transmit the value of our brand with "love" as the core.

Paperlux GmbH — Germany
076-079

The full circle of natural creativity is completed when the intuitive minds of 10 pioneering spirits from Hamburg's Schanzenviertel district perform their craft. Here is where inspiration, abstraction, passion, palpability and aesthetics are transformed into concept, branding, corporate and editorial design, event communication, typography, illustration and art. A surge of growth, an indelible imprint, a lasting impression.

Maxime Archambault — Cancda
080-089

Maxime Archambault is a graphic designer / illustrctor from Montreal, Canada. His body of work spans T-shirts, corporate identity and fine art. Traveling through different styles and mediums, Max's work is tied together by its tongue-in-cheek sense of humor and vibrant colours. In the past few years, his work has focused on T-shirt illustrations and men's street fashion. He has had the chance to design for Converse, Adidas, and several independent brands. His illustrations have won several awards, including the Threadless Challenge and the DesignByHumans competition. Max has also been featured in various books and magazines, including 3D Type Book and Digital Art. His illustrations and paintings have been shown in exhibitions around the world, including in Montreal, Beijing, Berlin and New York.

Anna Kozlenko — Ukraine
090-103

Anna Kozlenko young designer in Ukraine, She shares excellent illustration and document material on many platform websites.Her work is very practical with sub-style.

Ceci Lam — Hong Kong, China
104-113

Ceci Lam is an illustrator and animator based in Hong Kong. She graduated from Hong Kong Polytechnic University since 2014, but her passion lies in painting, drawing and handcrafting, which is what she truly excels in. Ceci enjoy her life and she loves to travel, and most of her images feature landscapes and people she has met on her journey. Also she wants to experience more and depict more stories she has invented in the future.
Web: www.behance.net/ceciilam

Guangzhou Guoguan Culture Communication Co., Ltd. — China
114-123

Guoguan, a brand which contributes to the crossover between art, culture and products, focuses on nourishing the soul through traditional cultural and warming people's hearts through good stuff. There're around 10 million followers in all the platforms of Guoguan and more than 200 famous brands work closely with Guoguan through the cooperation mode of Content + E-commerce. Moreover, Guoguan owns a very well-rounded supply-chain, strong sales forces and in the future, it will continue innovating and developing in the cultural industry.

Beatrice Tinarelli — Italy
124-133

Beatrice Tinarelli,also known as hellobea, was born in 1978 and lives in Bologna, where she works as a freelance illustrator and graphic designer. She deals with clients from all over the world and has mostly been published in the US and the UK children's books market. Her art is a colourful mixture of flat, humour, retro and vector style.

Jhonny Núñez — Colombia
134-143

My name is Jhonny Nunez, I'm a graphic designer and illustrator, born in southwestern Colombia and based in Russia now, my career is intercontinental scale, studying at the Institute of Fine Arts of Cali, Academy of Professional Drawing, design school Joso Tarragona and Scola. I am the captain of the ship called Jhonny Núñez - STUDIO, a modest space that provides services of graphic design and illustration international agencies like BBDO Sancho, Charlot Enterprise, Umer, Illozoo, Oxy among many others. I had the prestige of being hired by brands such as Microsoft, Unilever, Postobon, Norma, Victorinox, WeTransfer and other major brands. Among my professional awards are five Behance Apreciation YDB Award and a prize.

Aditya Pratama — Indonesia
144-153

Aditya Pratama (sarkodit) is an Indonesian illustrator who studied Communication Visual Design at National Institute of Technology, Bandung. He enjoys drawing in both traditional and digital media. Some of his works published on magazines, newspapers, website, ads, and books. The Last award received by him is Genkosha Illustration File Award 2015 (Japan). He also collects a lot of fiction and children book. And his favourite book is Abarat by Clive Barker.

Tommy Chandra   Indonesia
                                                  154-165

Tommy Chandra is a Pekanbaru-born now settles in Jakarta, Indonesia as an illustrator. Using his background in architecture and talent for design, Tommy creates amazing, clean, sleek, and stylish vector art. Inspired by everyday life, Tommy certainly loves geometries and all things vintage. Tommy has worked on numerous advertising and editorial commissions for national and international brands/clients. in 2012, Tommy built his own illustration and design studio, HEIMLO.
Web: tommychandra.com

Reda El mraki   UK
                                                  166-171

Reda El mraki's art is known as "Doodle Art" wich is a mix of funny colorful cartoon characters and shapes.

Rutger Paulusse   Netherlands
                                                  172-189

Rutger Paulusse is an illustrator based in Amsterdam, The Netherlands, focussing on designs for online and print, playing around with graphic shapes, bold colours, dimensions and space.

Guillaume Kashima   France
                                                  190-197

Guillaume Kashima is a French illustrator living in Berlin. He started his career as a graphic designer in advertising but later moved on to illustration. From this experience, he kept a direct and minimal approach of images as a vector of communication. His work today embraces different fields and medium such as prints, apps or objects. Guillaume 's work is also very versatile in terms of visual aesthetics, but his process always originates from boldness, wit and humour.

Musclebeaver   Germany
                                                  198-225

MUSCLEBEAVER are Andreas Kronbeck and Tobias Knipf, based in Munich/Germany. They work as a team in animation, illustration and graphic design since 2007.
www.musclebeaver.com

Enisaurus   Spain
                                                  226-235

Enisaurus is a full-time freelance Commercial Illustrator with a background in graphic design, currently working and living in Valencia, Spain. He loves drawing based on geometry, playing with intense colors and adding textures to his illustrations. Thinking in the right concept as the base of the meaning for each project is the main thing for him. A good thought idea builds a strong base to start the project and get the right intention and impact desire with it.
Enisaurus develops projects for helping companies, advertising agencies, magazines, books and private clients to communicate their services or products. Working on side projects is really important for Enisaurus, he is always trying to combine real commissions with his love for experimenting and making new stuff every month. He claims that there is not another way to evolve as an illustrator, for growing beyond your limits, learning from your mistakes and enjoying the success to reach your goals. His work is influenced by his love for movies, tv series, cartoons, books, comics, toys, video games and the pop culture from 80's until nowadays.

Hei lichee   China
                                                  236-251

Hei lichee is an artist and a curative cartoonist. The works have been translated into many versions, such as traditional Chinese and French and have been commonly accepted by readers. In 2005,the art brand 'Hei lichee' has been created and has been cooperated with Nike, Bvlgari, Converse, Huawei and other fashion brands, as well as on shelves, photography, design and other fields. It is the first Chinese author of the commercial installation exhibition on the theme of picture book. Now the theme works 'Flowers' series are being pushing out, which has slowly turned the Hei lichee into a more widely loved artist and has become a unique visual symbol.

Lantos Studio   China
                                                  252-287

The Lantos studio is one of China's most interesting culinary creative studios. They believe that food is emotional, memorable, and civilized. Therefore, they use everything in the world as food, and develop unedible grandiose cuisine. They also dig out the acting of each food, and direct an unrestricted visual blockbuster. In addition to his own creative design of food blockbusters, Lantos Studio also works with brands and companies that also advocate creativity, to incubate the beautiful and outrageous still life blockbuster, advertising\MV art, or brand image production. Here, vision and taste are illusions.

Wenju Chen   China
                                                  288-303

Wenju Chen, visual communication design graduation, two years of Japanese traveling, now mainly engaged in visual creative work. He likes to collect and read books and good at painting things cute.

Maomao cat stdio   China
                                                  304-313

Maomao cat studio was created by Mr. Yin Ge in 2011 and now located in Shijiazhuang. There are three people in the studio, mainly in the creation of Maomao cat cartoon, illustrative. Nearly ten works have been published. In 2017, the works are printed into T-shirts for online sales.

Kaa illustration   VietNam
                                                  314-319

Kaa illustration is a studio based in Ho Chi Minh since 2014 by two illustrators Phung Nguyen Quang and Huynh Kim Lien. We mostly do illustration for children's book. Our illustration inspired by the folk culture of Vietnam and Asia. You can see our illustration at www.kaaillustration.com.

Studio-Takeuma   Janen
                                                  320-365

Studio-Takeuma live in Kyoto with my wife, Japan. He graduated from Kyoto Institute of Technology. His illustration and design are full of fun and metaphor. He is good at computer-generated vector illustrations, and his account painting is full of artistry.

ACKNOWLEDGEMENTS

DESIGNERBOOKS (DB) sincerely thanks all the artists, designers and companies that contributed to this book, meanwhile thank all the staff, translators and printing companies involved in the design and production of this book. Without their efforts and contributions, the book will not be presented to readers in a graceful manner. We will pay attention to all the valuable suggestions from all our friends, and DB will make every effort to do well in every book.

JOIN US

If you want to join DESIGNERBOOKS for future projects and publications, please submit your work and information to edit@designerbooks.com.cn.